Famous Lute Solos

Arranged for Plectrum Guitar

Rob MacKillop

To access the online audio recording go to:
WWW.MELBAY.COM/31059MEB

The 2020 Legacy Concerto Ce acoustic guitar image is courtesy of Breedlove Guitar Company.

WWW.MELBAY.COM

Contents

Title	Page	Audio
Introduction	3	
A Toye (Anon)	8	1
Dove Son Quei Fieri Occhi (Anon)	9	2
Draw near me and love me (Anon)	10	3
Pezzo Tedesco (Anon)	11	4
Se lo M'accorgo (Anon)	12	5
Volte (Anon)	13	6
Menuet 1 BWV 1006a (J. S. Bach)	14	7
Prelude in Dm BWV 999 (J. S. Bach)	16	8
Sarabande BWV 996 (J. S. Bach)	20	9
Sarabande BWV 995 (J. S. Bach)	22	10
Tastar de corde (Dalza)	23	11
Orlando Sleepeth (John Dowland)	24	12
What if a Day (John Dowland)	25	13
Fantasia 2 (Drusina)	26	14
Alman (Robert Johnson)	28	15
Ricercare 1 (Spinacino)	30	16
Ricercare 2 (Spinacino)	32	17
Fantasia in Em (S. L. Weiss)	34	18
Prelude in Em (S. L. Weiss)	39	19
Tombeau sur la Mort de M. Comte de Logy (S. L. Weiss)	42	20
About the Author	47	

INTRODUCTION

I have played these pieces on Renaissance and Baroque lutes, and in arrangements for classical guitar. I have also spent decades of my life playing acoustic guitars with a pick/plectrum. After making these arrangements, I'm convinced that this great repertoire can also be played by intermediate-level plectrum players, but not only that: they sound great on steel strings too!

Technique

Obviously, it is possible to play two-note chords (called dyads) on adjacent strings, but with careful practice it is possible to play dyads on non-adjacent strings:

Although it is possible to play the second C♯ on the 2nd string, in the flow of a performance it works better on the 3rd string.

The finger on the 3rd string just needs to lean back a little to briefly mute the 2nd string.

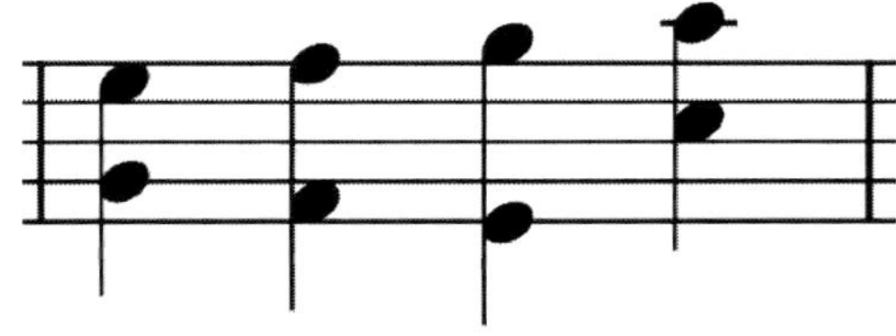

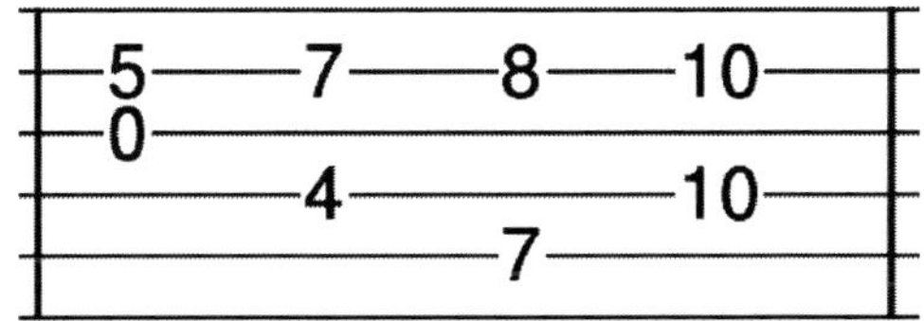

Here is an example with three types of dyads: adjacent, close non-adjacent, and wide non-adjacent. In the latter case, you need to mute two strings between the notes. It is perfectly possible to do this with a bit of practice.

However, in some instances the result can be a little distracting, or just really awkward. In those situations, I have employed either one of three options.

1. Separate the notes very quickly:

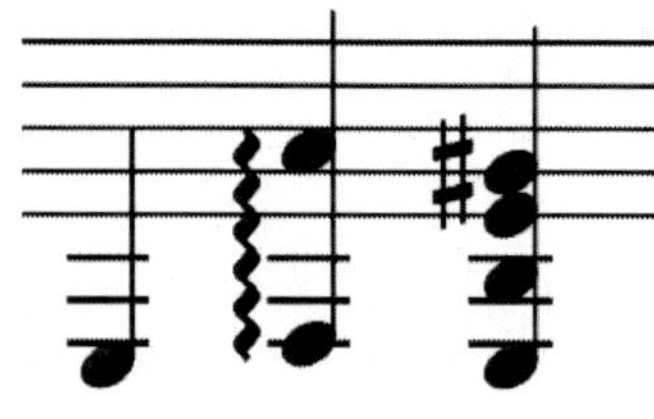

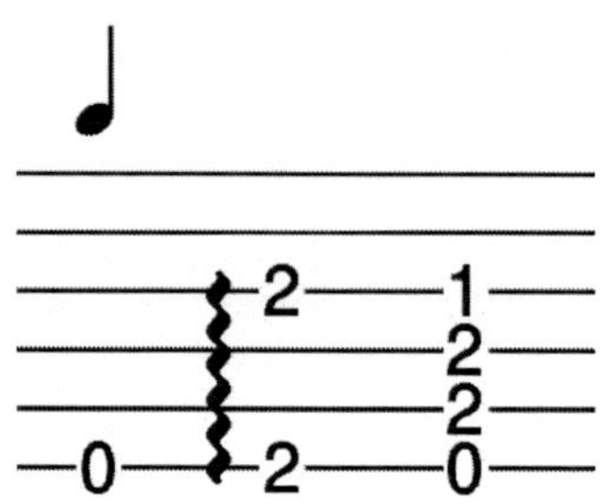

Here it is difficult to mute the 5th and 6th strings effectively, so I have suggested a quick separation of the notes, referred to as *separé* by French luthistes in the 17th century.

2. Fill in the chords with extra notes:

Here the first chord consisted of only three notes, on the 5th, 4th and 1st strings. As the second chord is originally a five-note chord, the music lost nothing by expanding the first chord to five notes also.

3. Hybrid picking

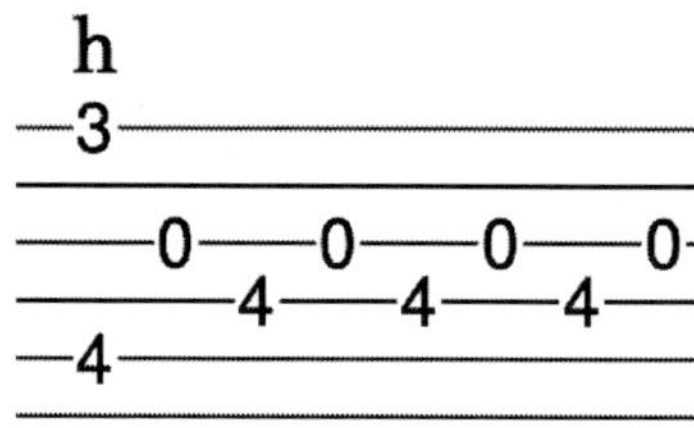

One more technique is known as "hybrid picking", where the plectrum plays the lower note of the dyad, while the middle or ring finger plays the upper note – both notes can be on widely-spaced strings, yet sound at the same moment. I indicate this technique with the letter h above the tab number.

COMMENTARY

Anon - A Toye: An enjoyable start to proceedings. I have filled in a few chords. Note that the chords used – A, D and E majors – are chords I, IV and V in the key of A. Many Renaissance dance pieces are based on this "three-chord trick" common to Blues music!

Anon - Dove Son Quei Fieri Occhi: Oscar Chilesotti (1848 - 1916), an Italian musicologist, copied items from a now lost lute manuscript. Thanks to his endeavors, we would not know these sublime pieces. A translation of the title could be; "Where are those proud eyes?".

Anon - Draw near me and love me: A beautiful Scottish lute piece from the Pickeringe manuscript. Jane Pickeringe had nothing to do with the compilation of the Renaissance pieces in the manuscript that now bears her name.

Anon - Pezzo Tedesco: Another beautiful piece from the *Chilesotti Collection*, which required a little judicious filling-in of some of the chords. The title means "German Piece".

Anon - Se Io M'accorgo: The third and final piece I have chosen from the *Chilesotti Collection.* A translation of the title could be: "If I Notice".

Anon - Volte: An Italian dance found in a 17th-century Scottish lute manuscript, the *Rowallan.* There is a version of this tune in the *Chilesotti Collection*, but with a repeated bass line which is impossible to play with a plectrum while also playing the other parts. Nevertheless, this is an enjoyable version to play.

Bach - Menuet 1 BWV 1006a: Here begins a small collection of Bach pieces from his lute series. The lute suites proved less fruitful for plectrum playing than the cello suites. See my *Bach Cello Suites for Plectrum Guitar* (Mel Bay Publications, 30978) for all six suites arranged for plectrum technique. Nevertheless, I'm sure you'll enjoy playing these four pieces.

Bach - Prelude in Dm BWV 999: A famous and popular arpeggio prelude by Bach offers an excellent workout for your right hand.

Bach - Sarabande BWV 996: The sublimely beautiful Sarabande from the "First Lute Suite". Try to let the music float in the air.

Bach - Sarabande BWV 995: The 5th lute suite of Bach was also arranged or composed (arguments rage about which came first, the lute or cello version) for the cello. The latest research points to the *violoncello da spalla*, as being the intended instrument for the cello version; this very large viola-like instrument, which was played under the chin. This piece sounds deceptively simple, yet it is far from easy to perform well.

Dalza - Tastar de Corde: From one of the earliest lute books at the dawn of the Renaissance, Tastar de Corde is a form of prelude. The title could mean "Feel, taste or touch the strings", and has an improvisatory quality. Lute players of the day were adept at improvising preludes, and we are fortunate that some were written down for future generations to admire and copy.

Dowland - Orlando Sleepeth: Here is the first of two short pieces by the great John Dowland. Notice the change of time signature halfway through, from 4/4 to 6/4. In each case there are two main beats per bar – the time signature consisting of the letter C with a line through it indicates 4/4 with two main beats, sometimes called "cut time". So, when the time signature changes to 6/4, maintain the same tempo of two main beats to the bar.

Dowland - What If a Day: A simple, largely chordal version of Dowland's popular setting of "What if a day, or a month, or a year", a poem by Thomas Campion.

Drusina - Fantasia 2: I'm particularly pleased that this piece by Benedict de Drusina (c.1520 - after 1573) works well with plectrum technique. You can view a video of me playing it on a Renaissance lute online.

Johnson - Alman: A popular composition which works well with a plectrum, with only a few chords filled in. The composer worked for William Shakespeare, providing the music for some of his plays at The Globe.

Spinacino - Ricercare (1): Two early Renaissance pieces by Francesco Spinacino from 1507. His two lute books from that year are the earliest lute publications. As with Dalza's "Tastar de Corde", Spinacino's music has a very improvisatory feel, and is rather daring in its mode shifting devices. Note the many scale passages; playing the lute with a plectrum (a feather quill, or piece of bark) had been the main technique of the Medieval period, and was still common when Spinacino's revolutionary books were published.

Spinacino - Ricercare (2): If you find one or two odd-sounding notes, don't worry, Spinacino is just grabbing your attention! Welcome to the sound world between the Medieval and Renaissance eras.

Weiss - Fantasia in Em: We finish with three pieces by the greatest lute player of the Baroque era, Sylvius Leopold Weiss. This famous fantasia is in two parts: a largely arpeggiated introduction leads to a quasi-fugue-like section which, despite a few tricky moments, works well for plectrum technique, and is enormous fun to play.

Weiss - Prelude in Em: Originally in Dm, this arpeggio-based prelude brings to mind the Bach “Prelude in Dm” which also appears in this book. Both pieces are a great workout for your plectrum-hand technique.

Weiss - Tombeau sur la Mort de M. Comte de Logy: We finish with one of the finest lute compositions of any era, the famous Tombeau (tomb-related elegy) written by one lute player after the death of another. The only real difficulty is the chord at the start of the second measure, but if arpeggiated (as intended by the composer) you don’t need all fingers down in advance. Even a split second can help you get the fingers in place. Notice the “wide vibrato” in measures 12 and 26. This is formally known as *bebung*, a trembling vibrato, common to the clavichord.

Rob Mackillop
Edinburgh
2021

A Toye

Pickering Lute Book

Arranged by
Rob MacKillop

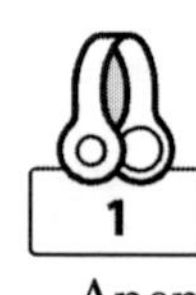

Anon

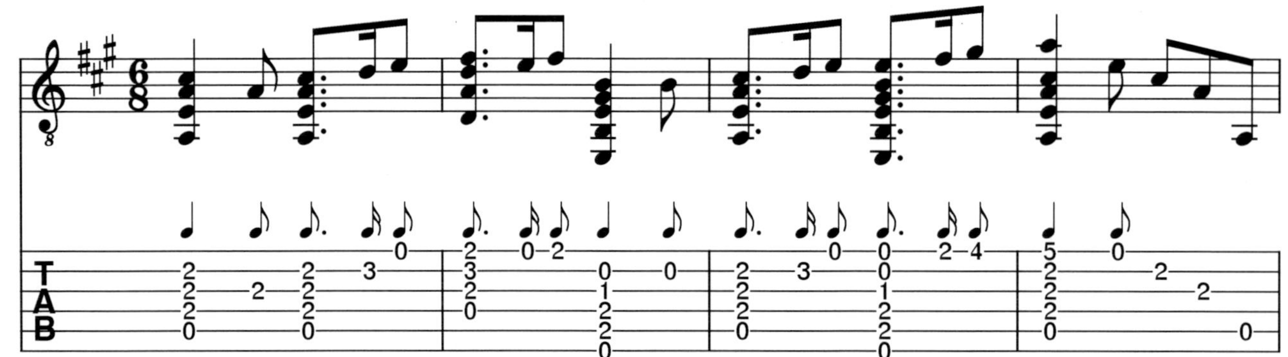
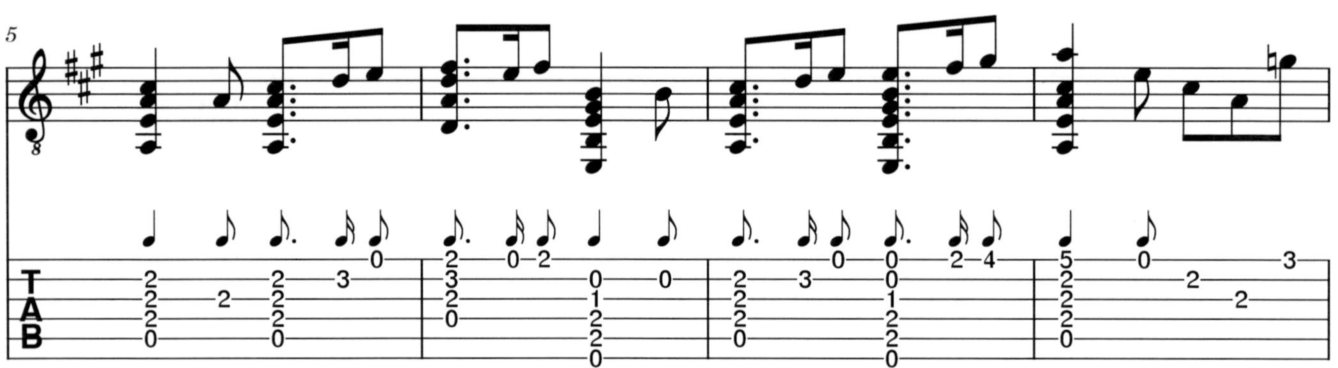

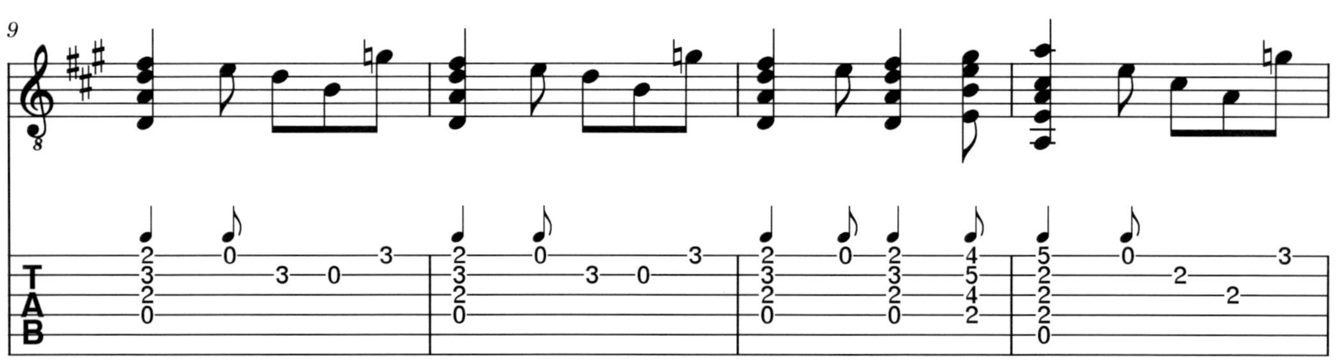

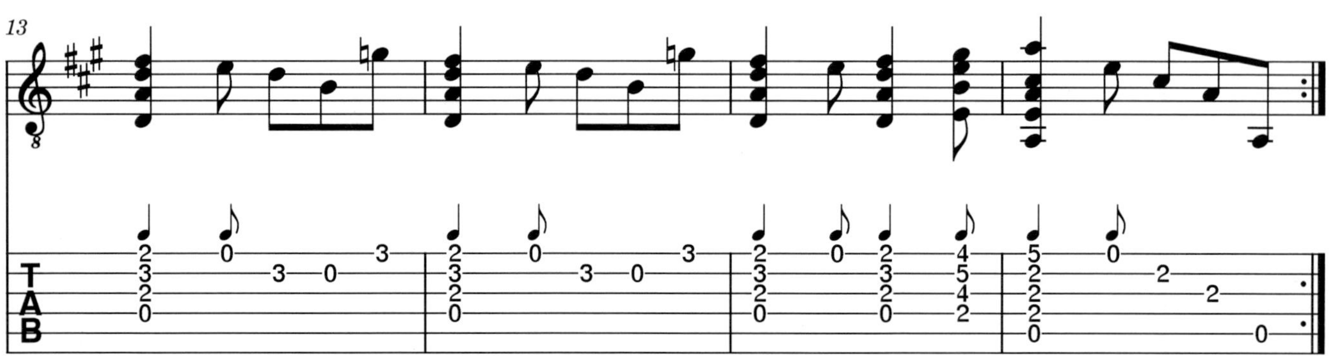

Dove Son Quei Fieri Occhi

Chilesotti Collection

Arranged by
Rob MacKillop

2

Anon

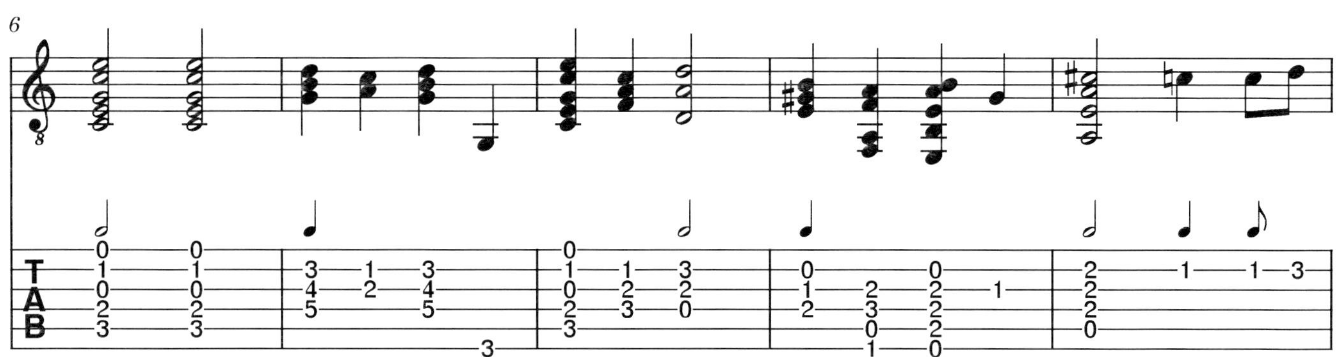

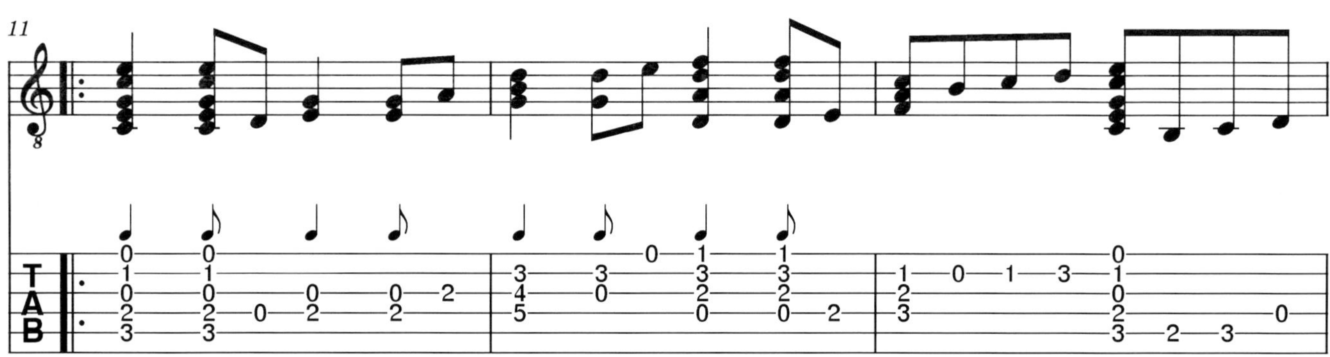

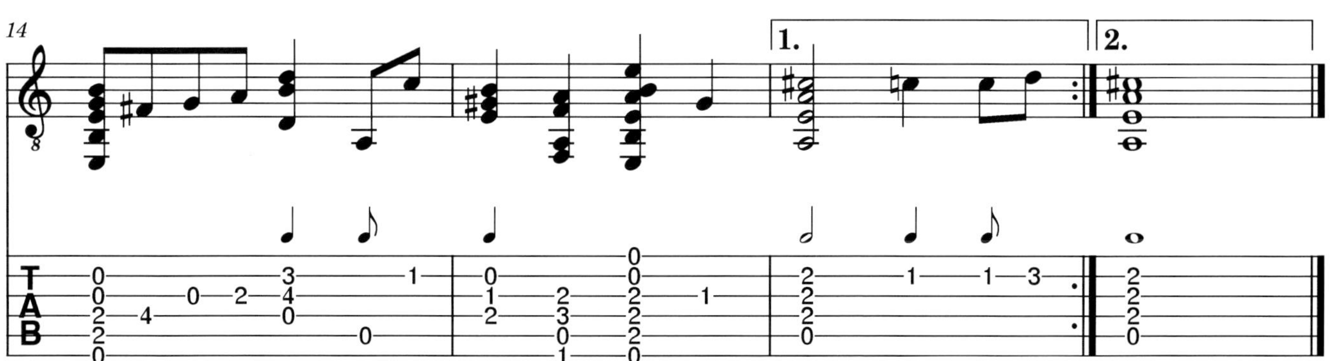

Draw near me and love me

Pickeringe Lute Book

Arranged by
Rob MacKillop

3

Anon
Scottish

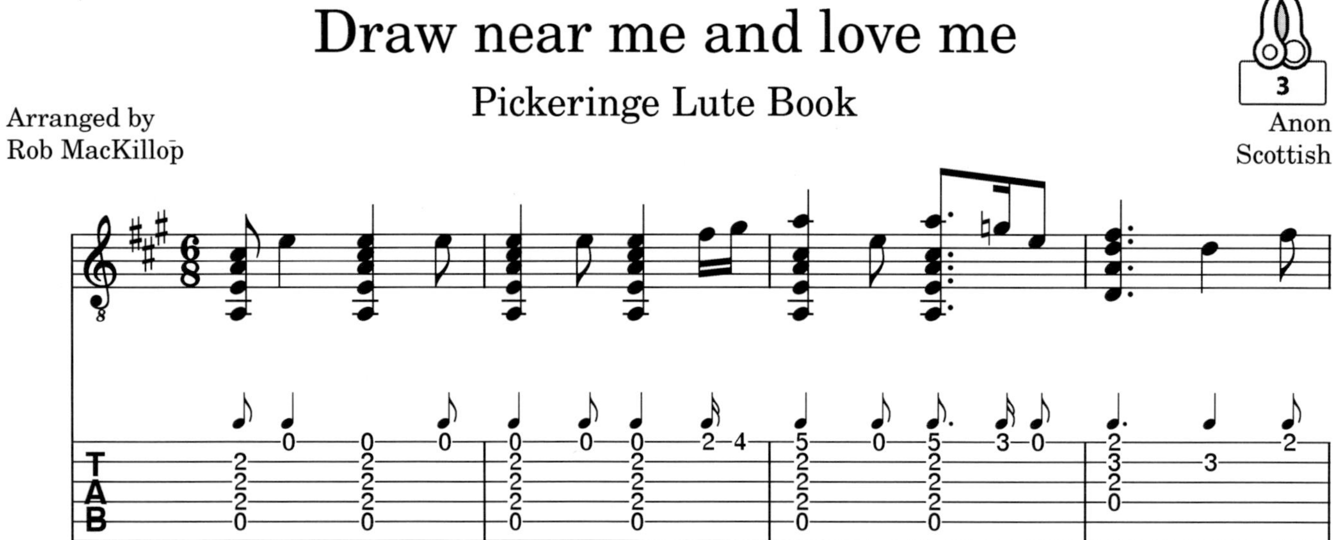

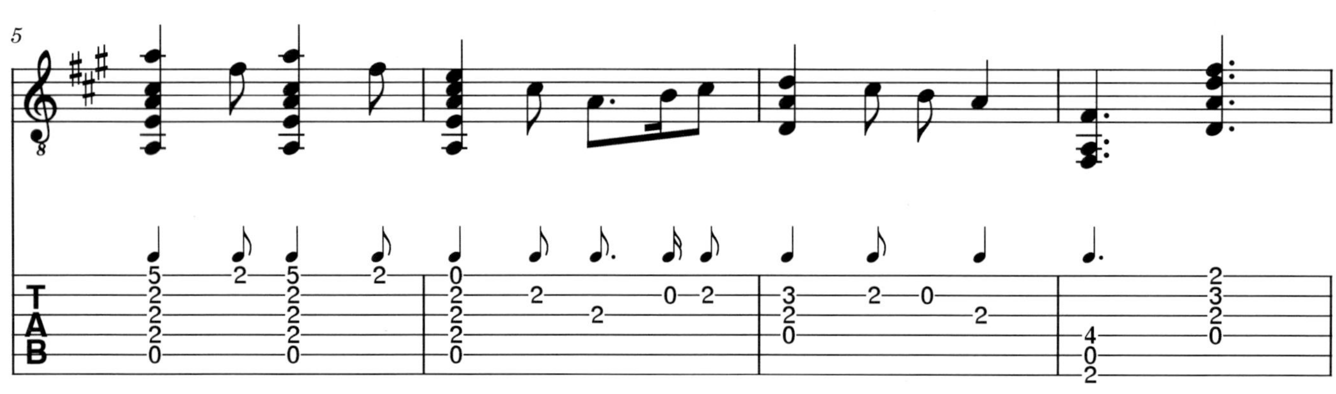

Pezzo Tedesco

Chilesotti Collection

Arranged by
Rob MacKillop

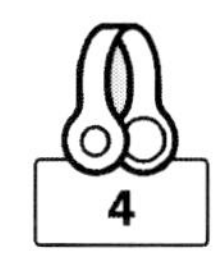

Anon

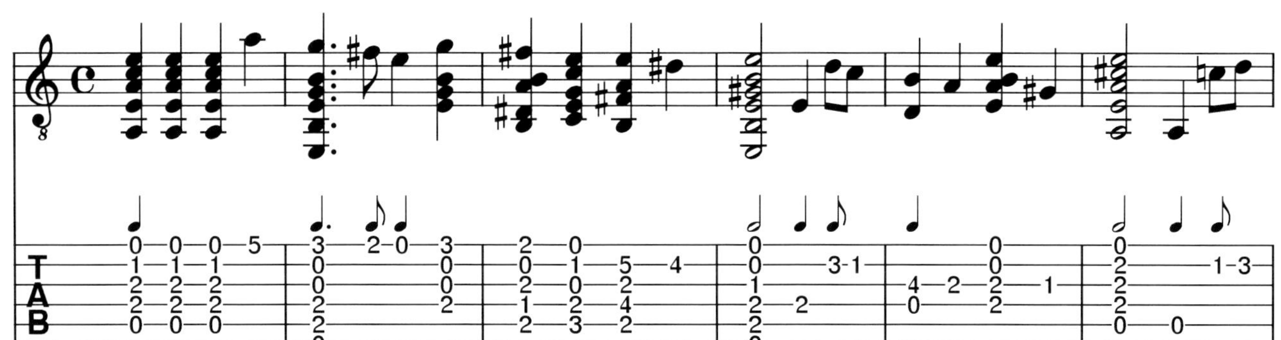

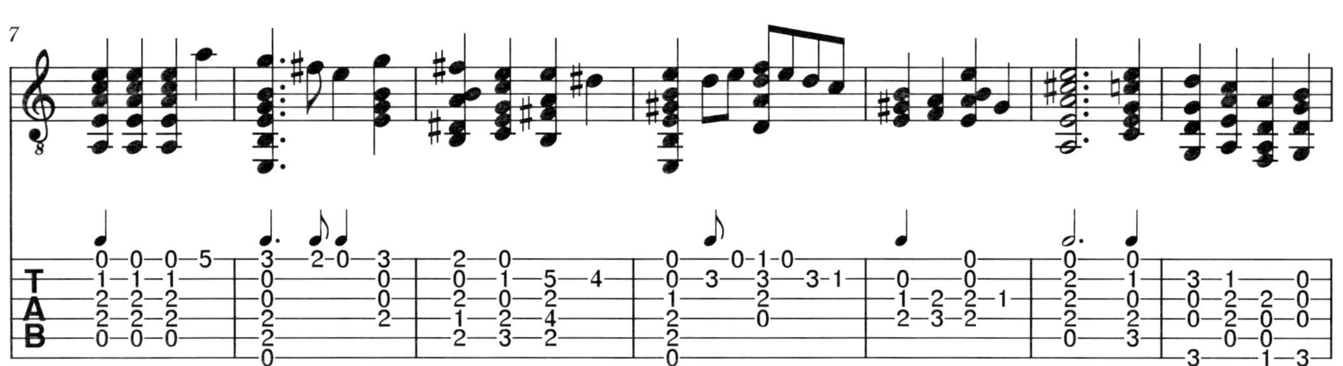

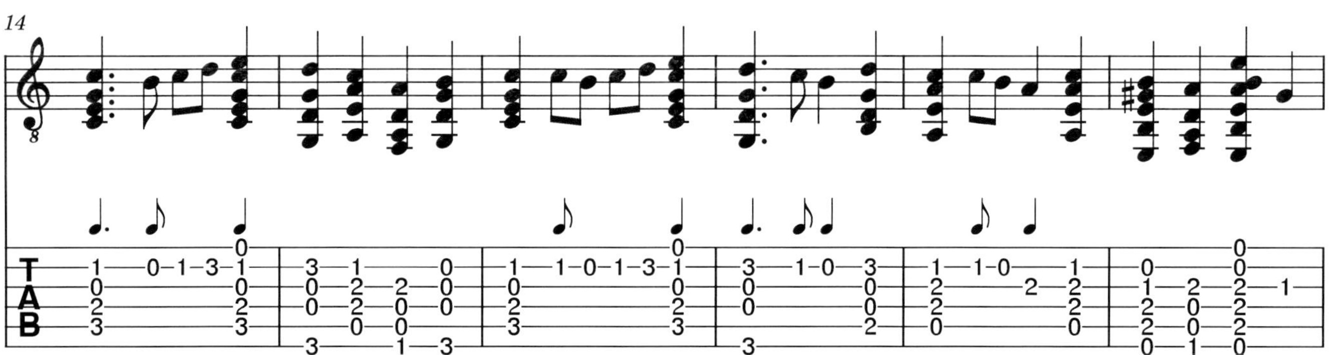

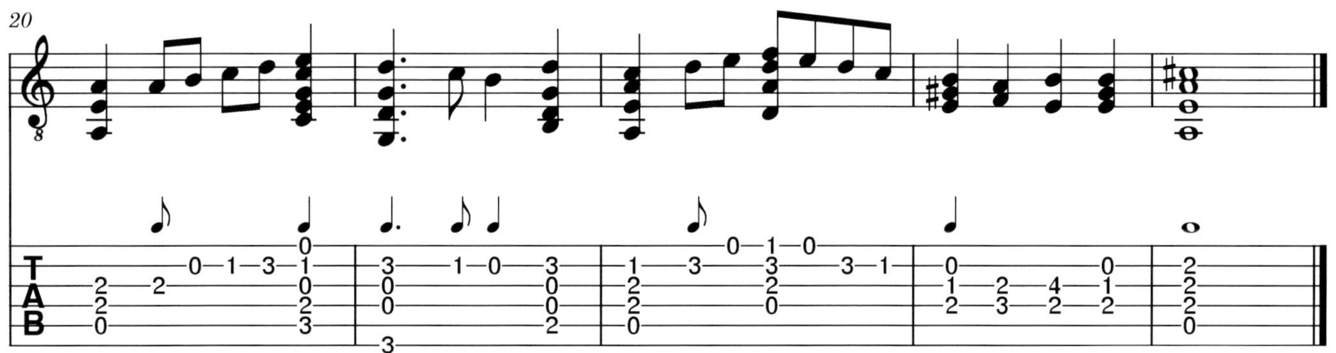

Se Io M'accorgo

Chilesotti Collection

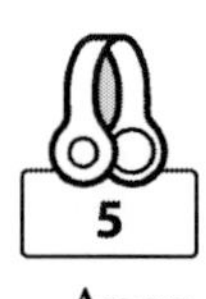

Arranged by
Rob MacKillop

Anon

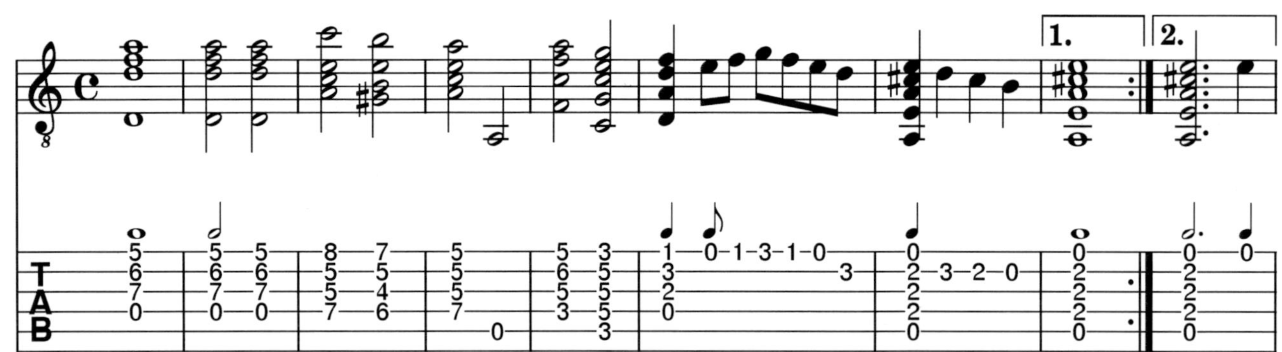

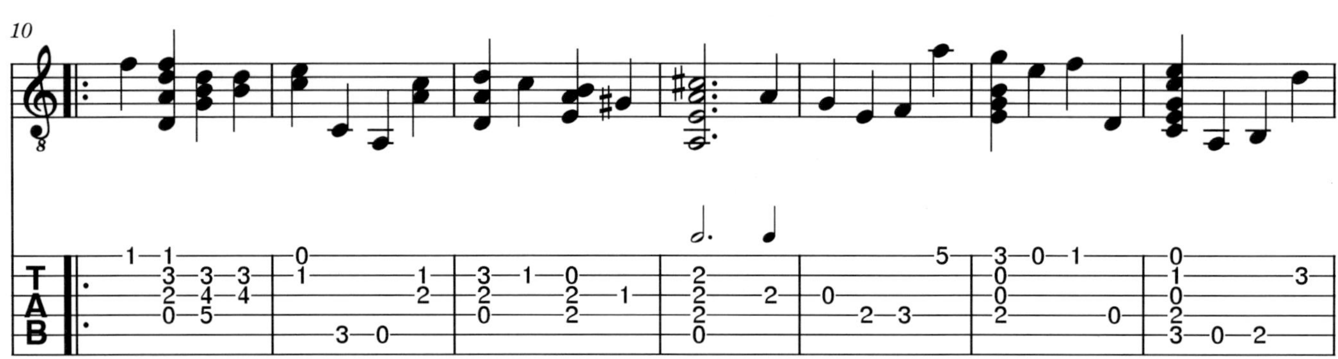

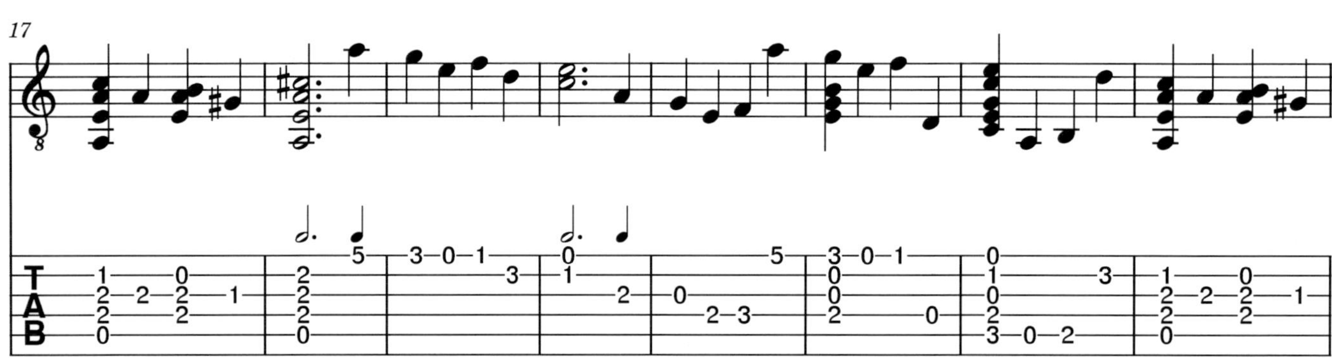

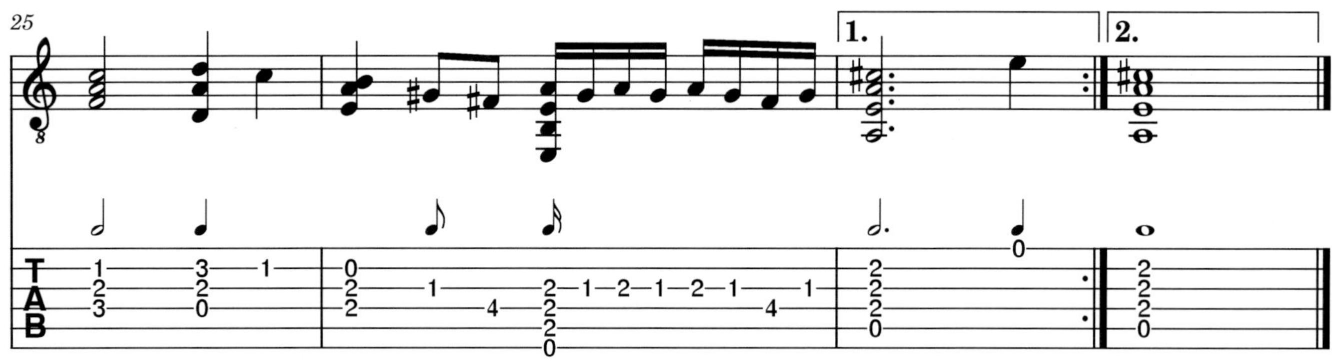

Volte

Rowallan MS

Arranged by
Rob MacKillop

6

Anon

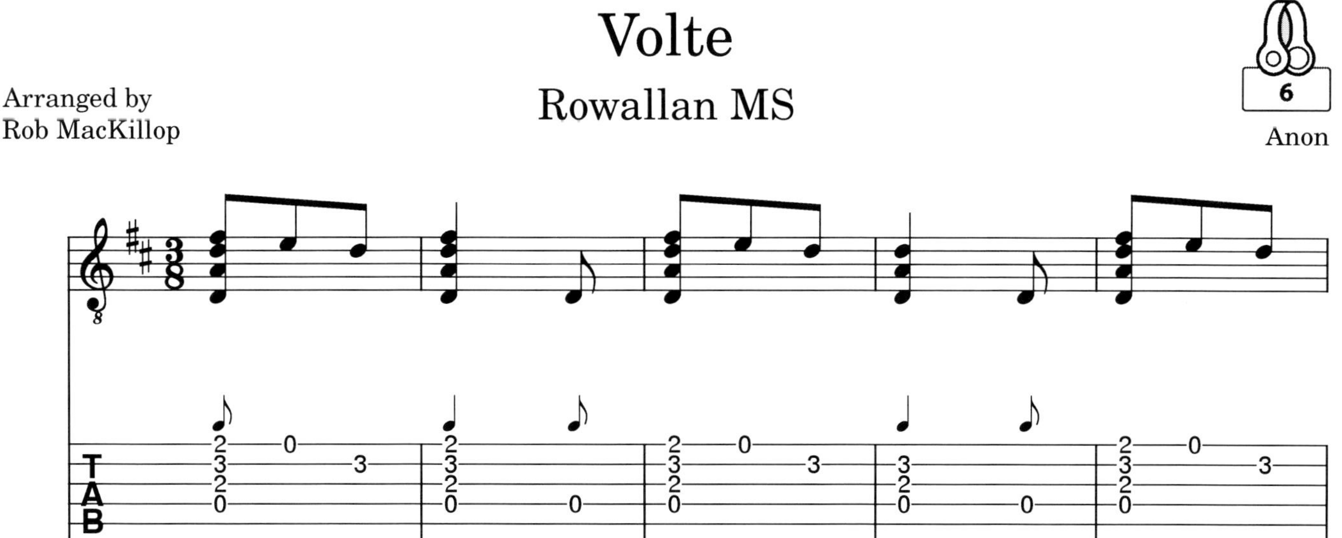

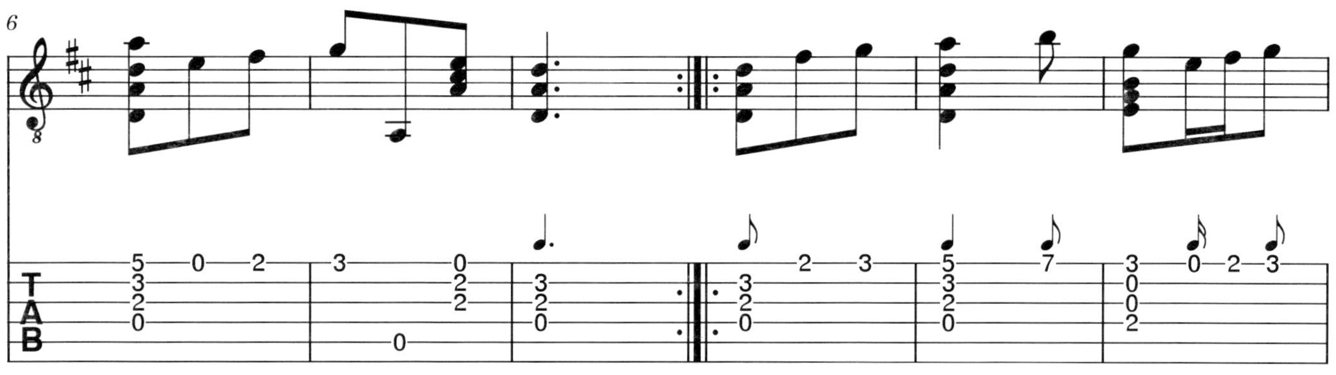

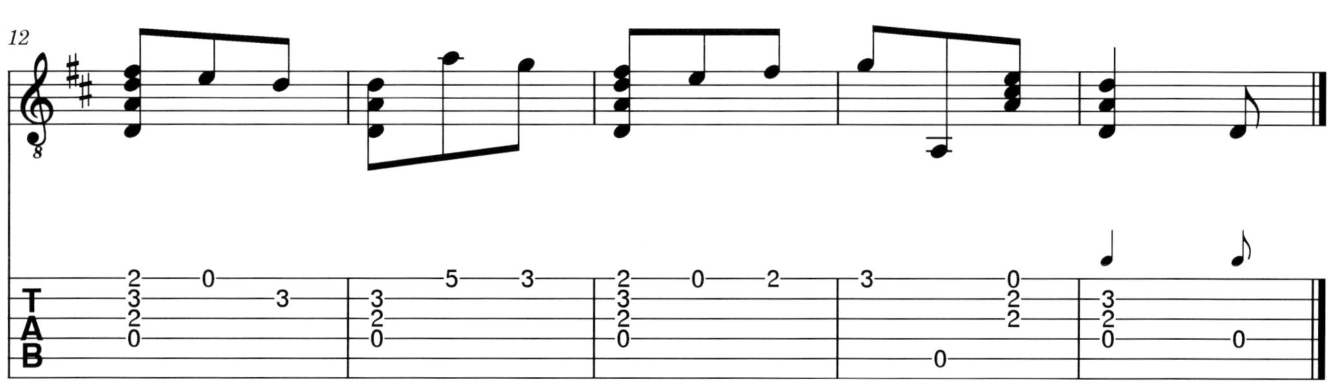

Menuet 1

4th Lute Suite, BWV 1006a

Arranged by
Rob MacKillop

J. S. Bach

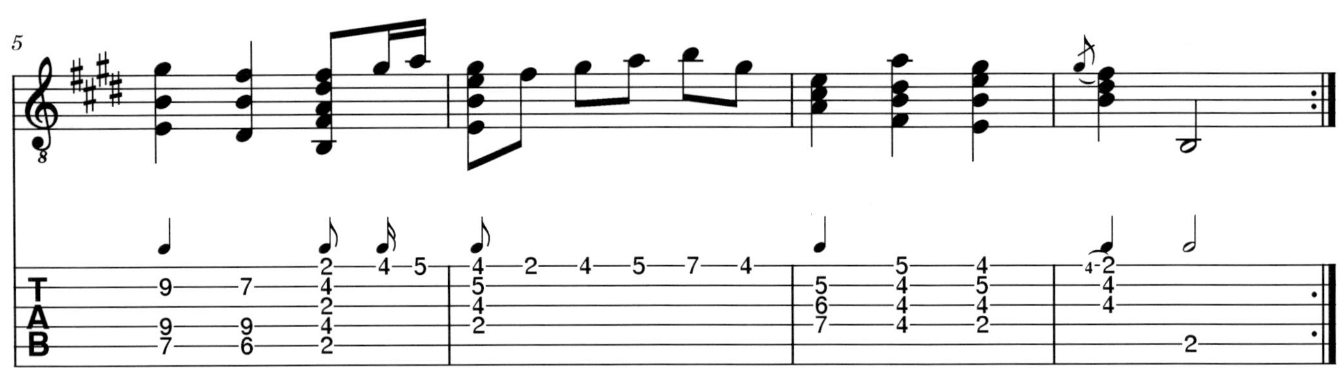

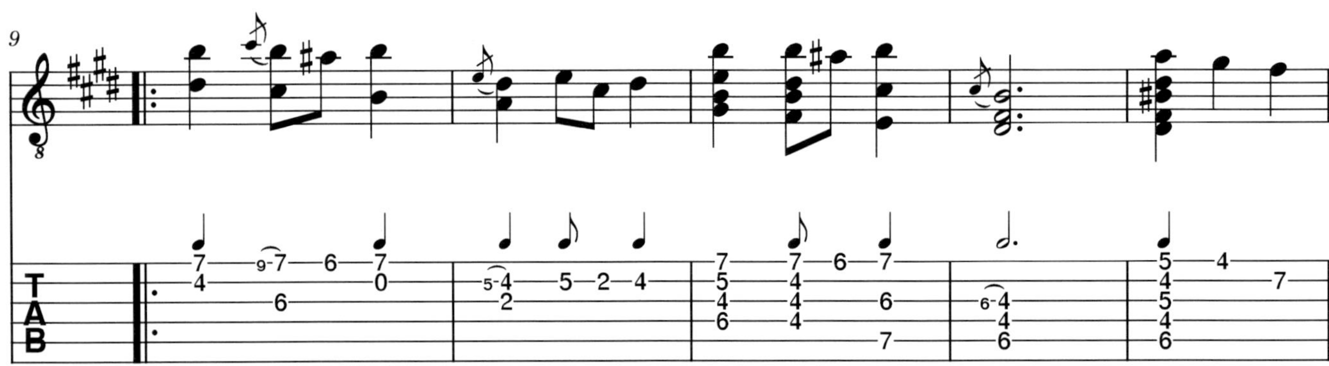

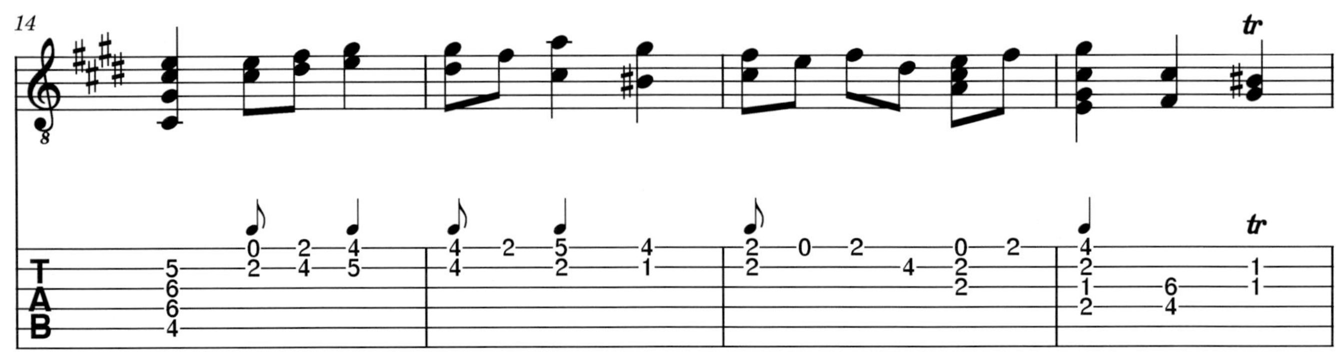

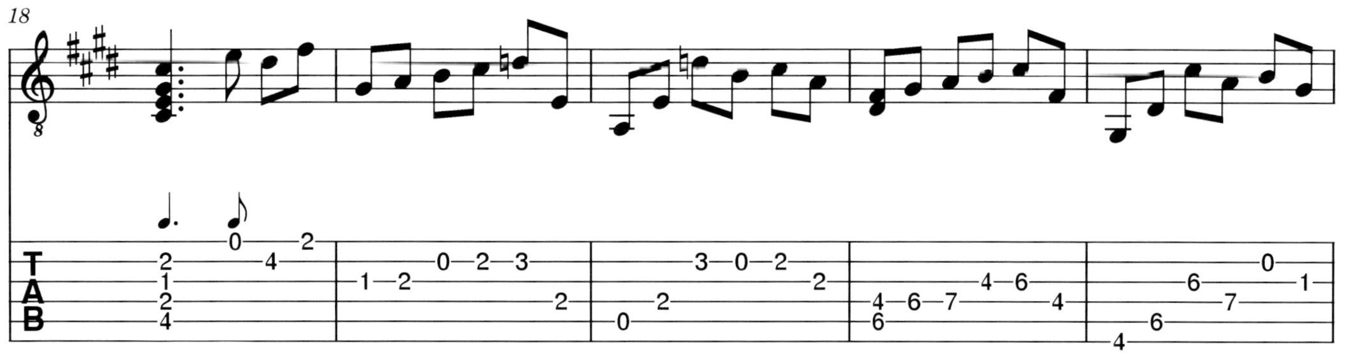
18

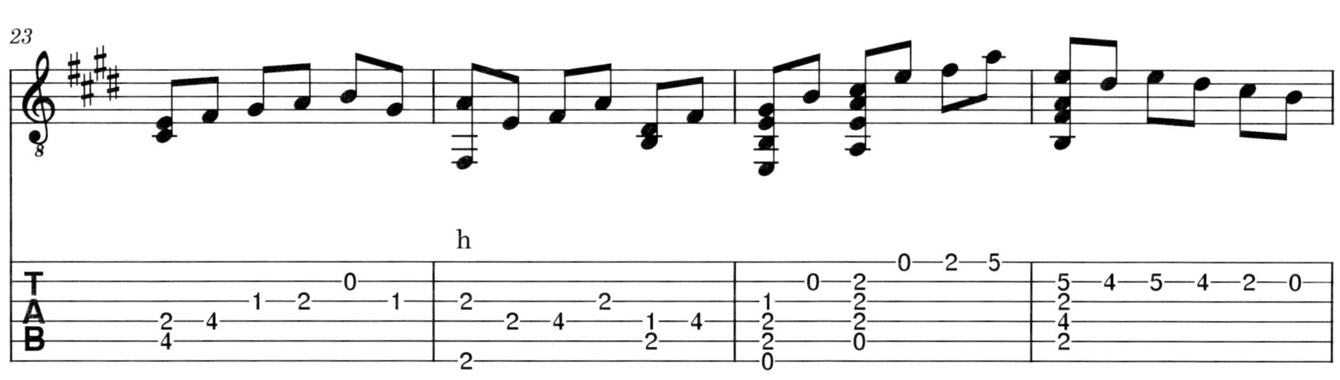
23
h

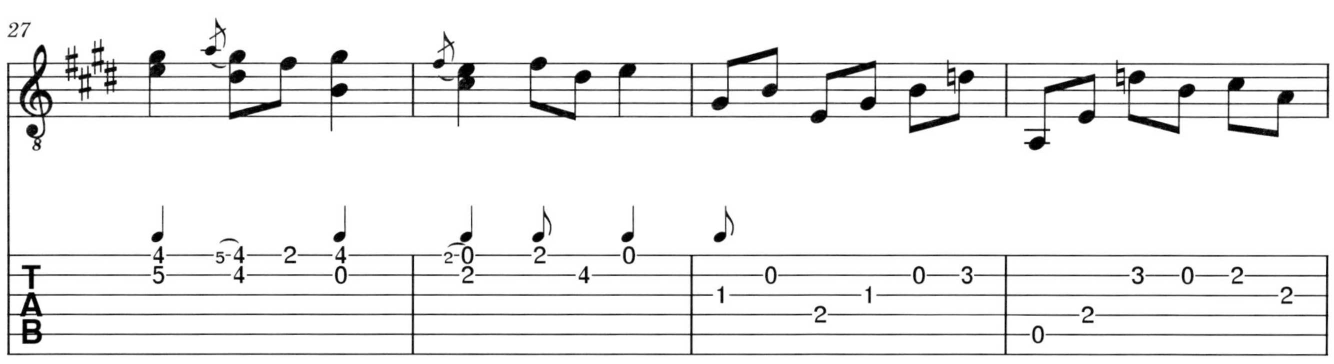
27

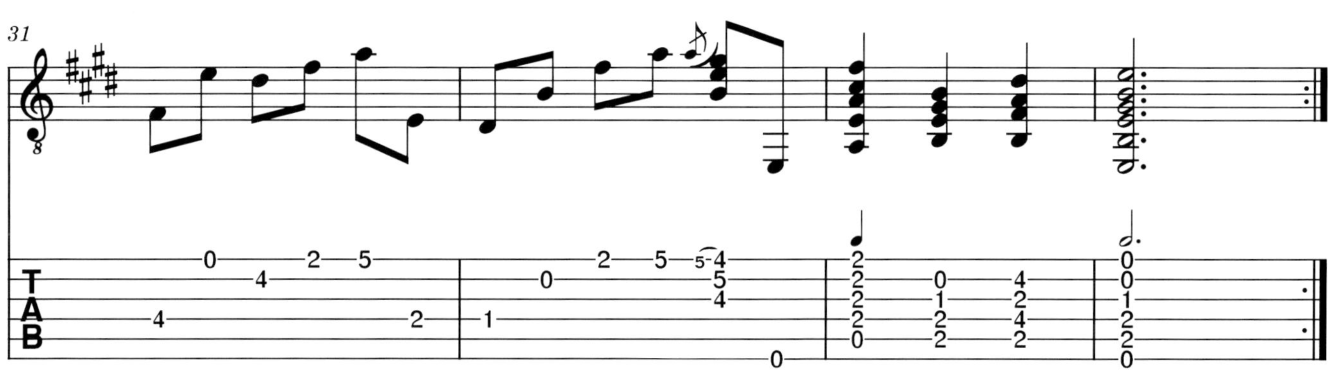
31

Prelude in Dm

BWV 999 [Originally in Cm]

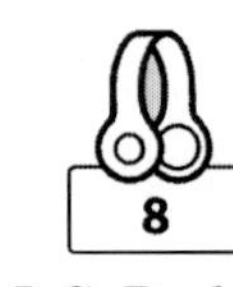

Arranged by
Rob MacKillop

J. S. Bach

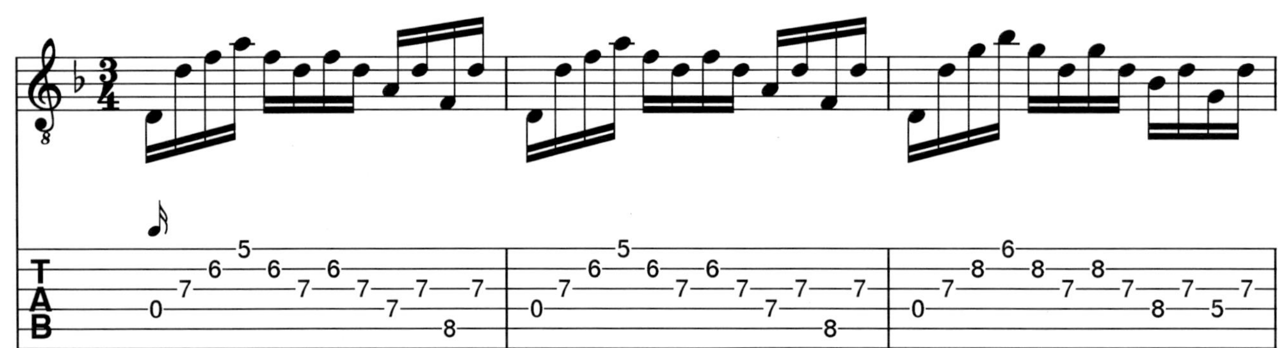

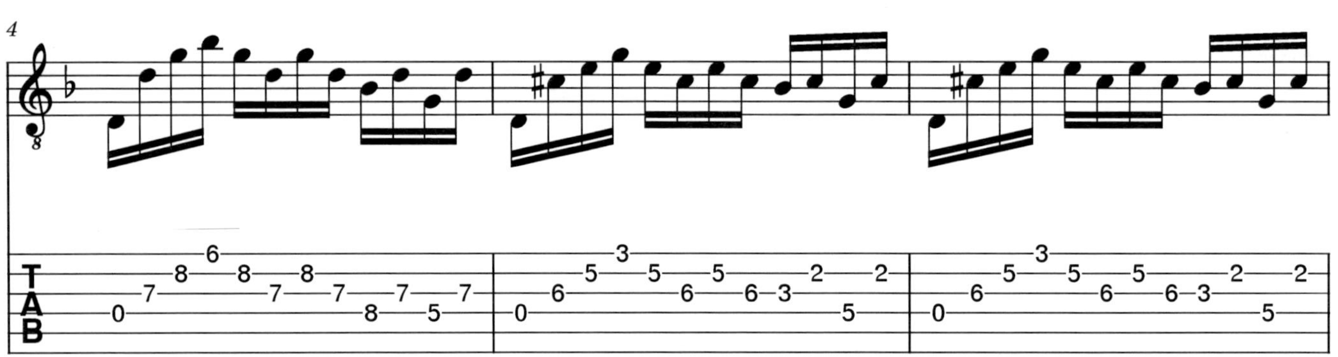

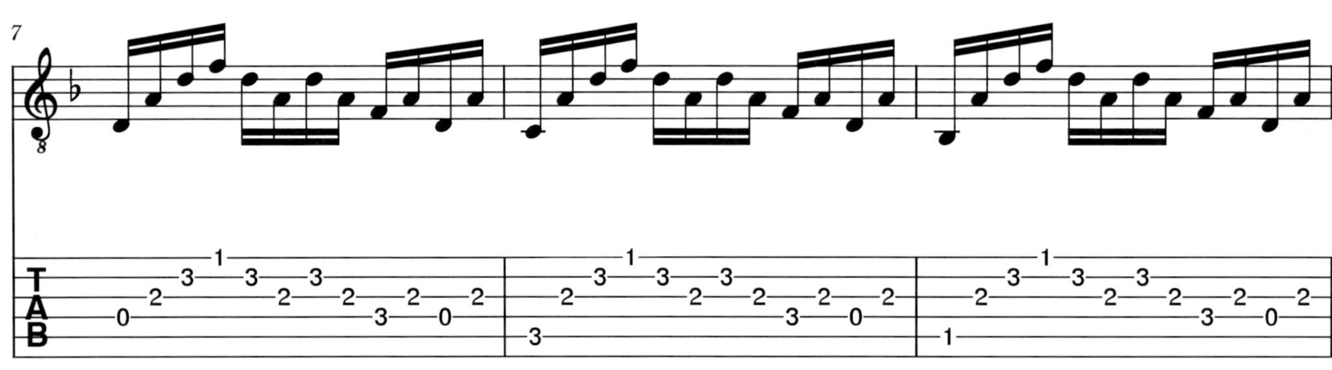

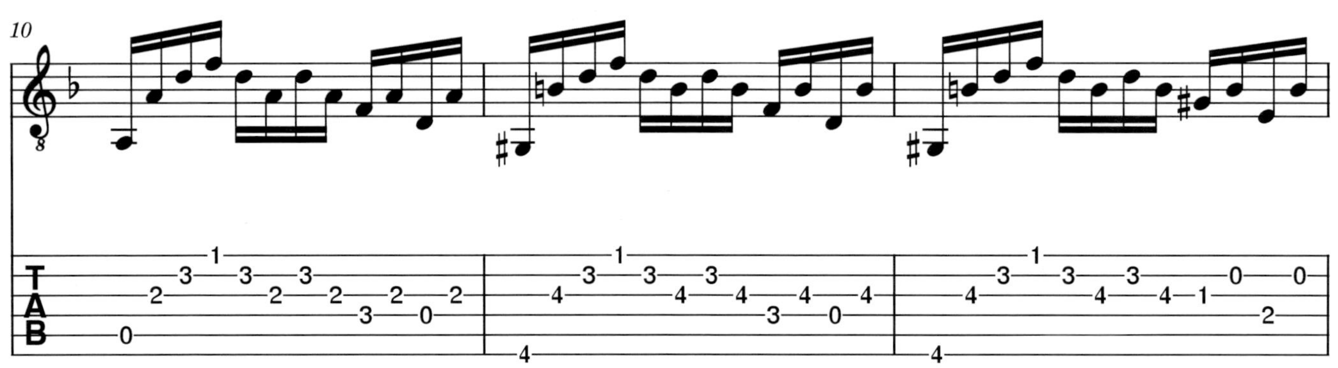

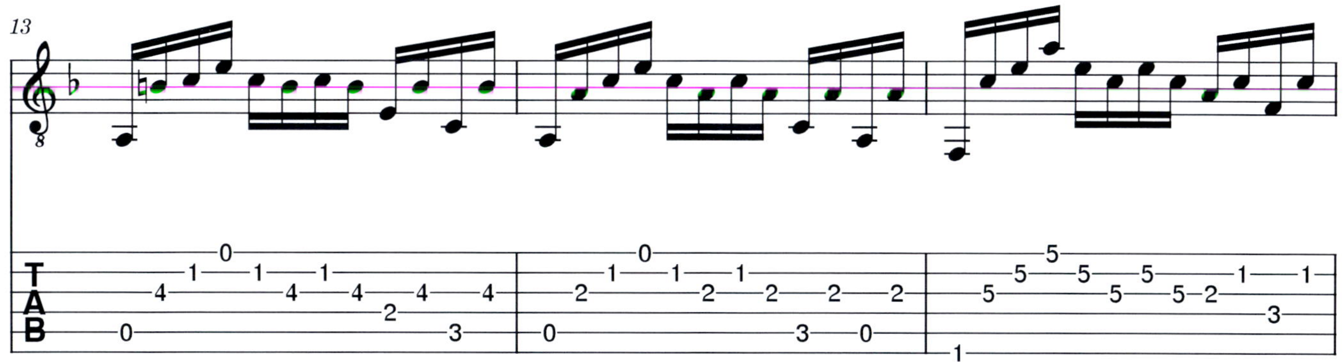
13

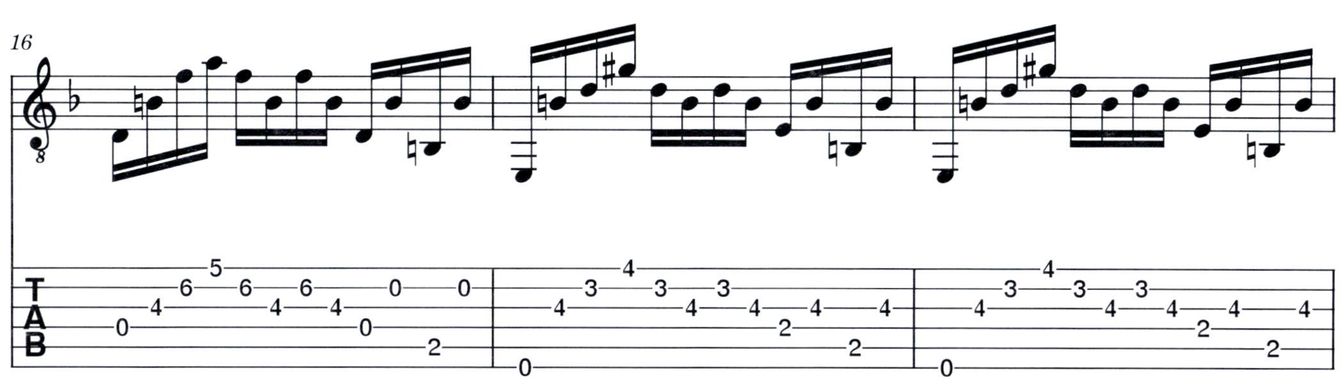
16

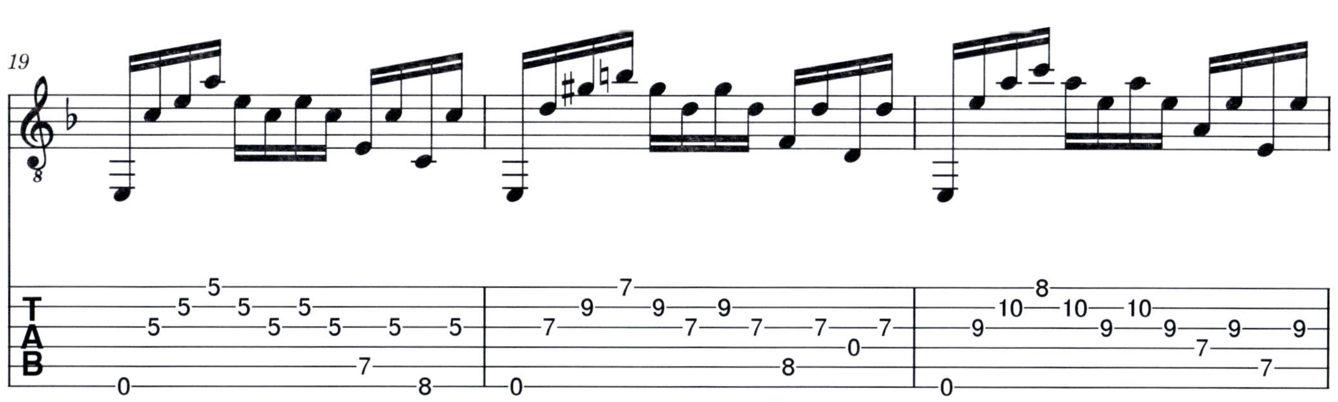
19

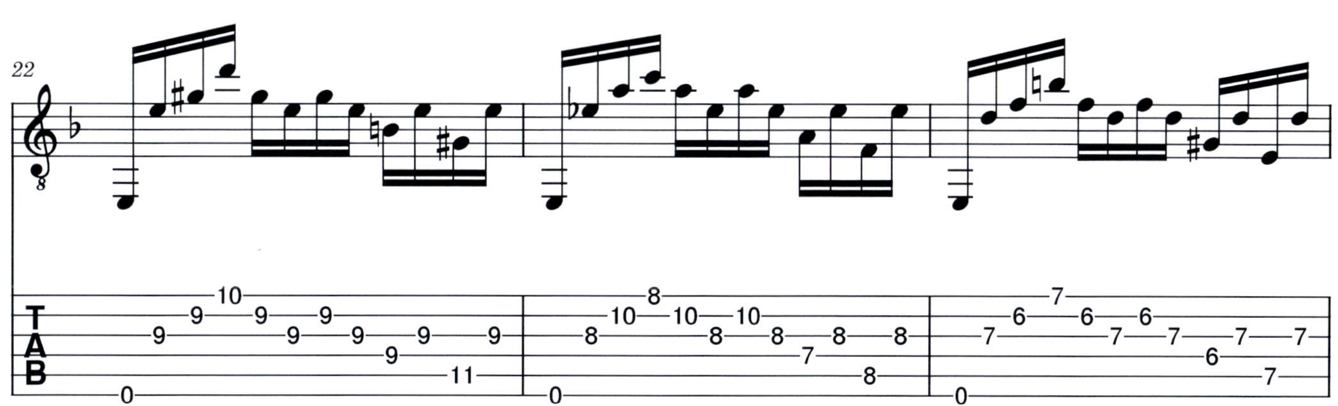
22

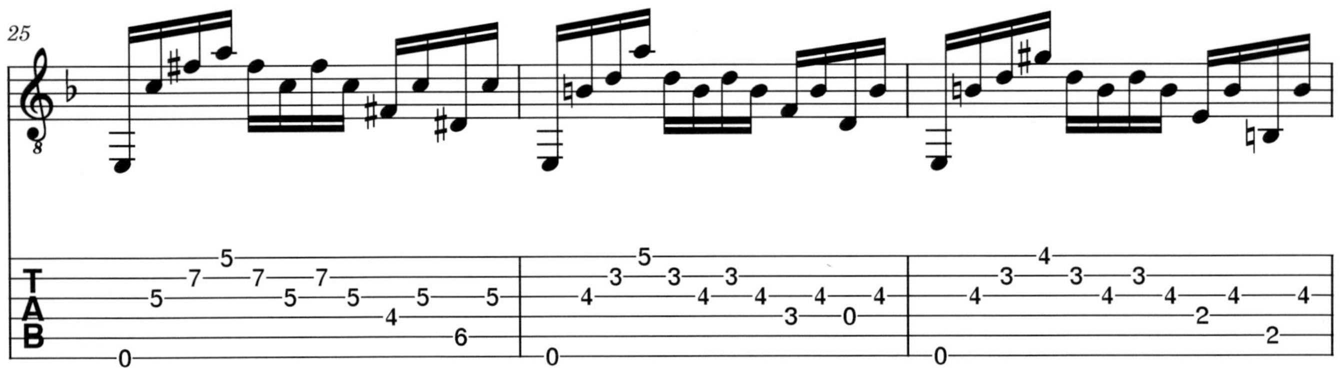
25

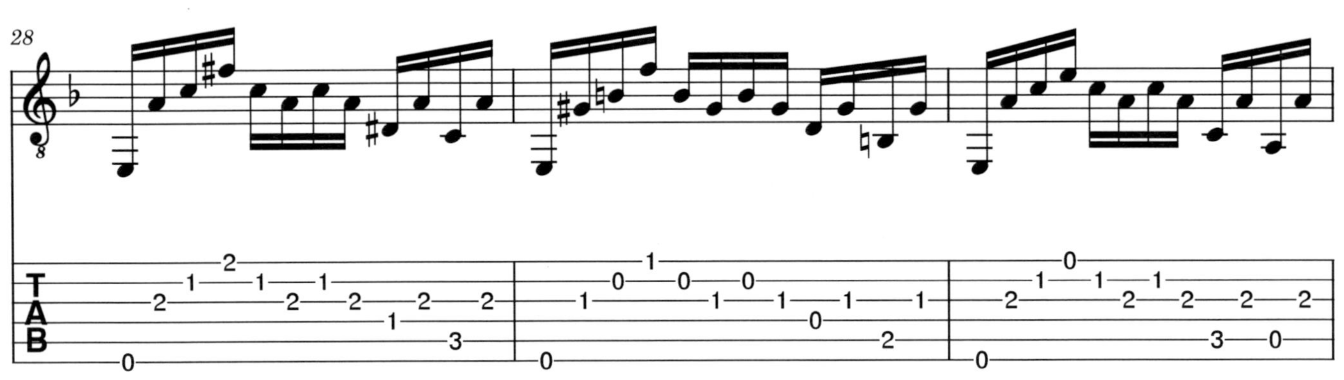
28

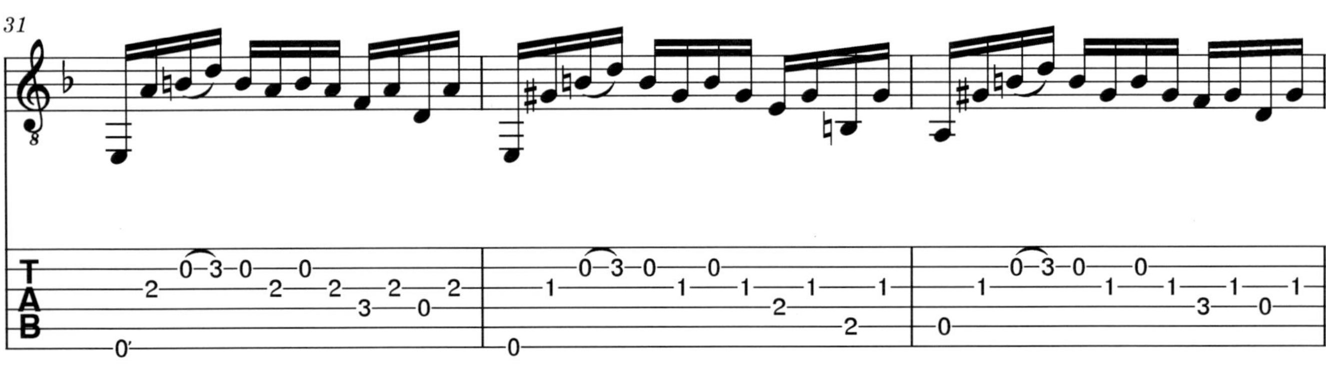
31

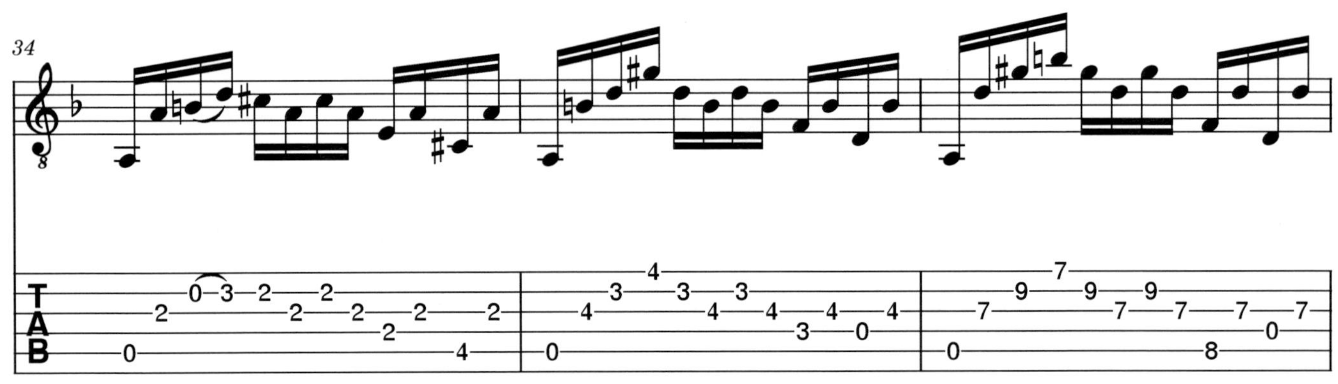
34

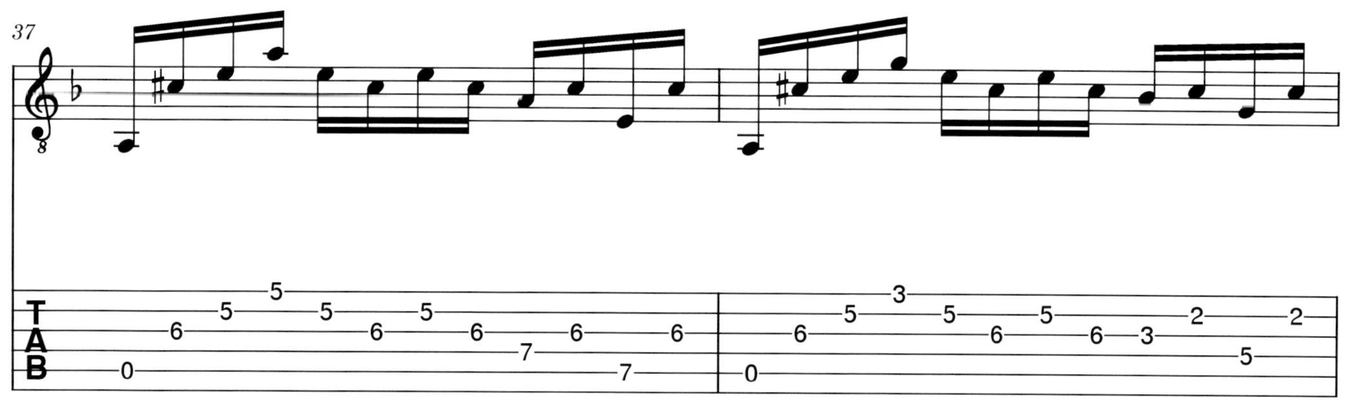
37
T
A
B

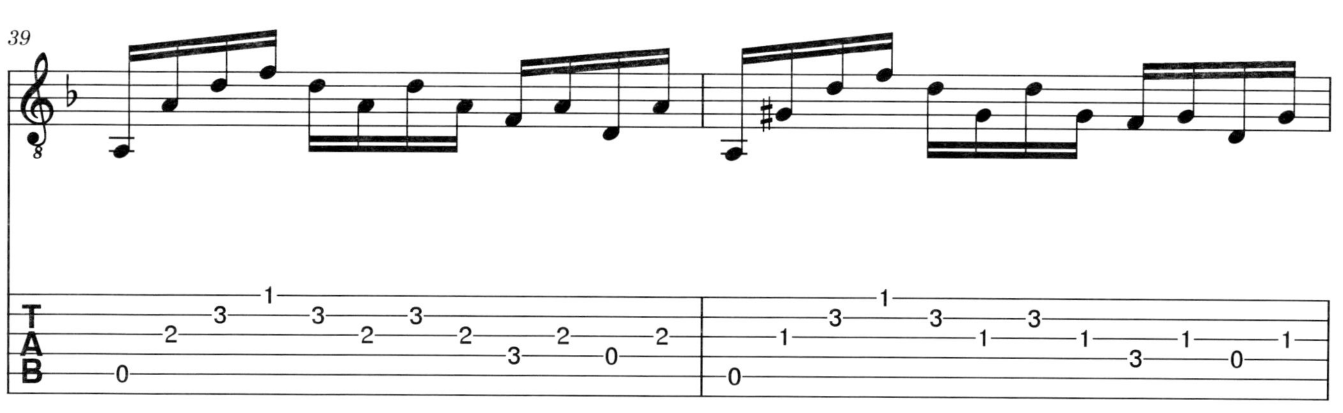
39
T
A
B

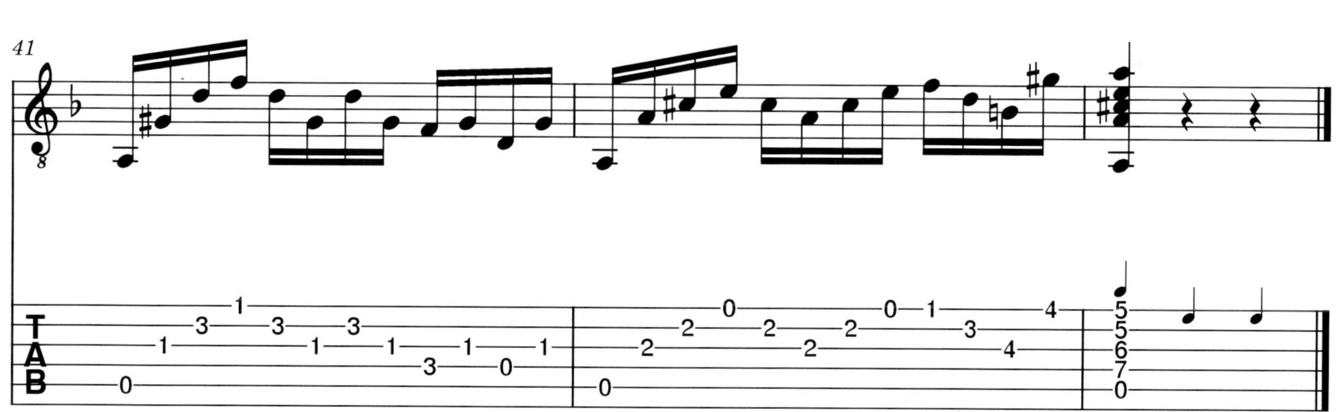
41
T
A
B

Sarabande

1st Lute Suite, BWV 996

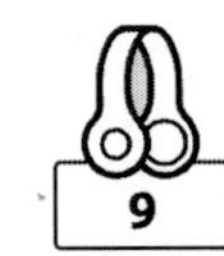

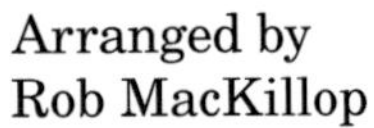

Arranged by
Rob MacKillop

J. S. Bach

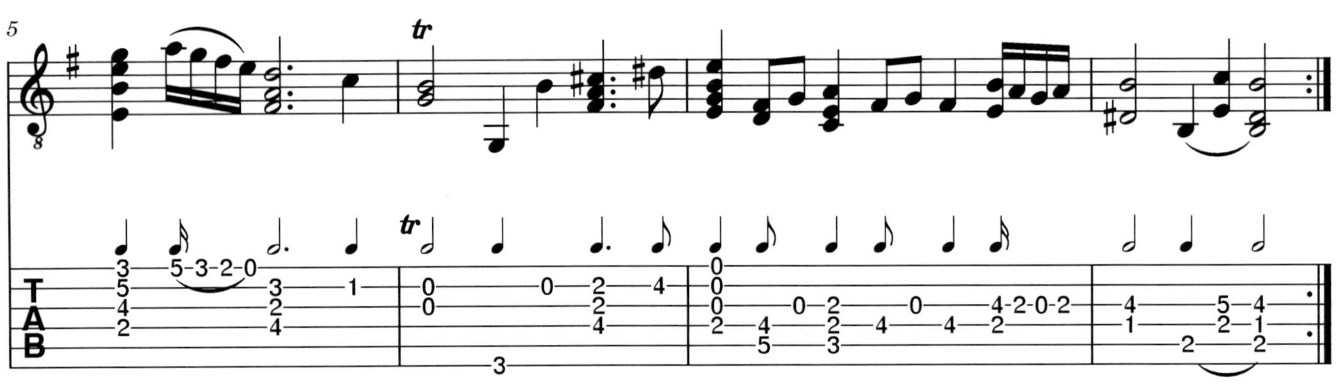

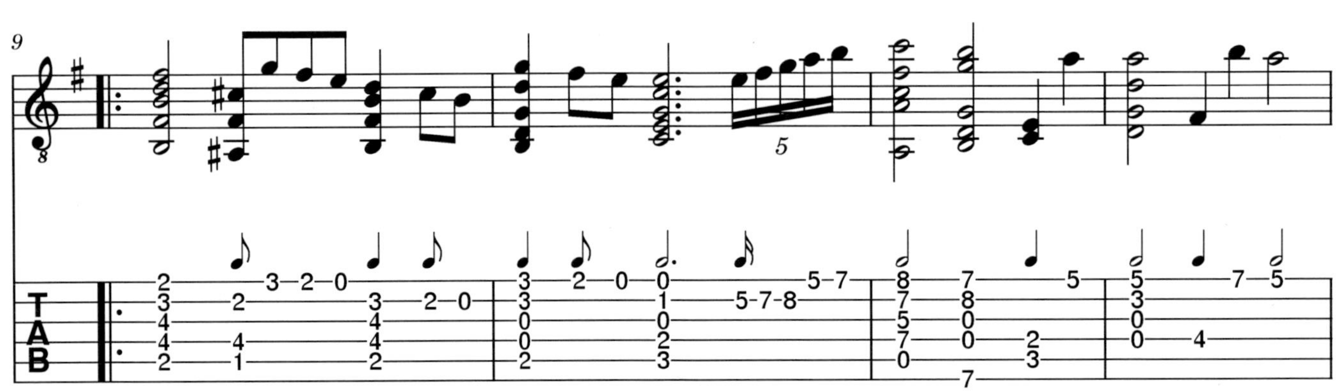

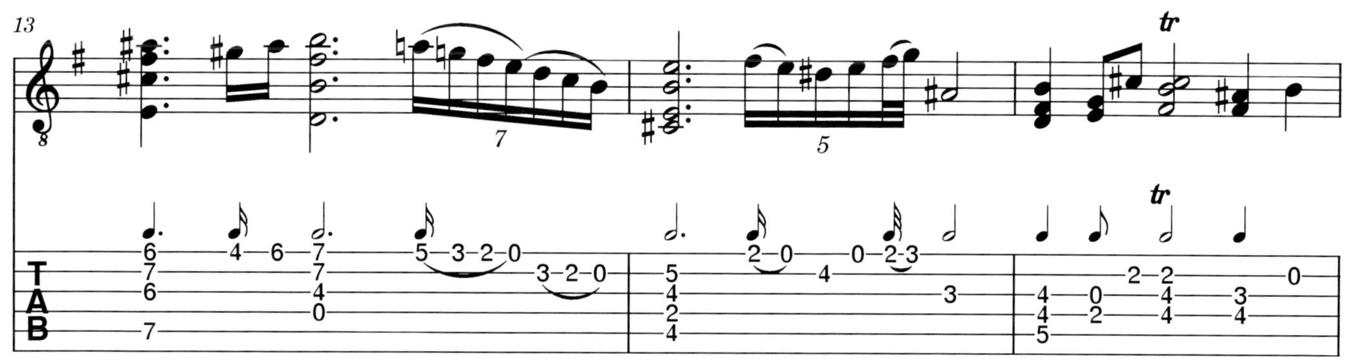
13
tr
tr
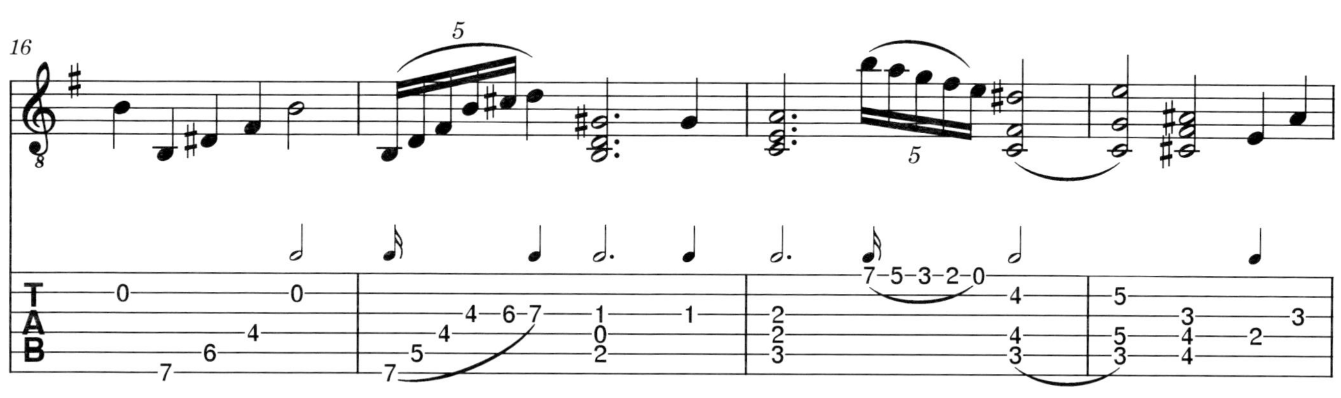
16

20
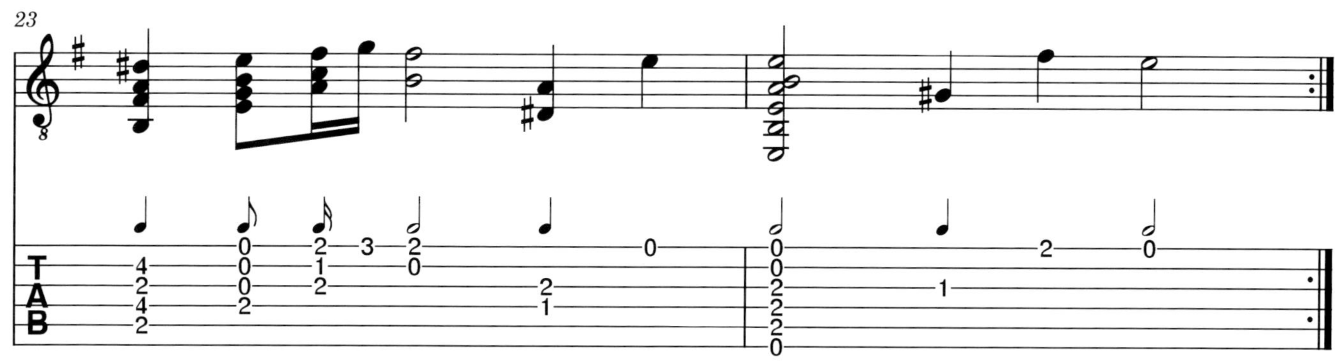
23

Sarabande

5th Lute Suite, BWV 995

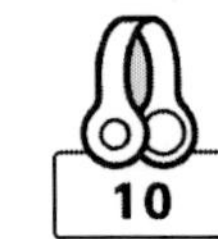

Arranged by
Rob MacKillop

J. S. Bach

Tastar de corde

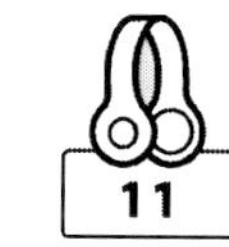

1508

Arranged by
Rob MacKillop

Joanambrosio Dalza

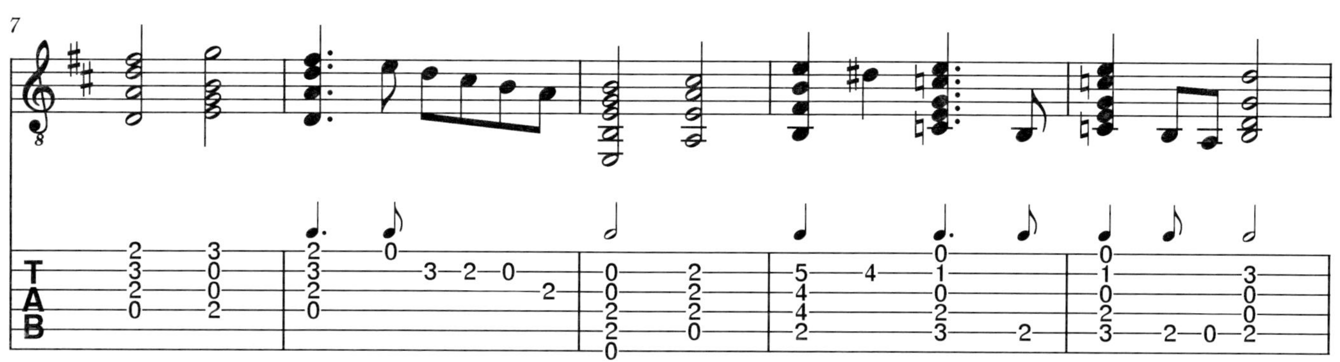

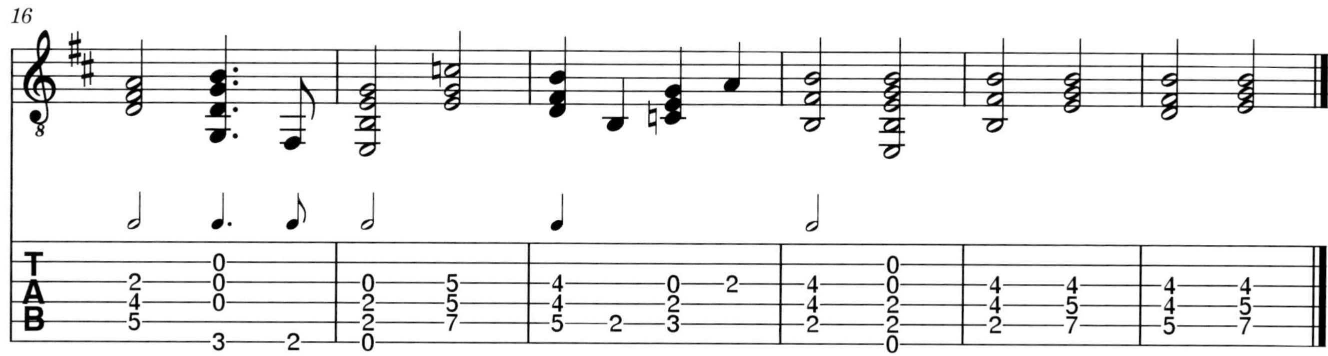

Orlando Sleepeth

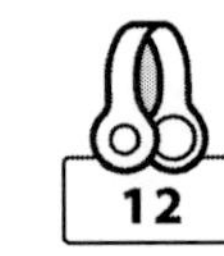

Arranged by
Rob MacKillop

John Dowland

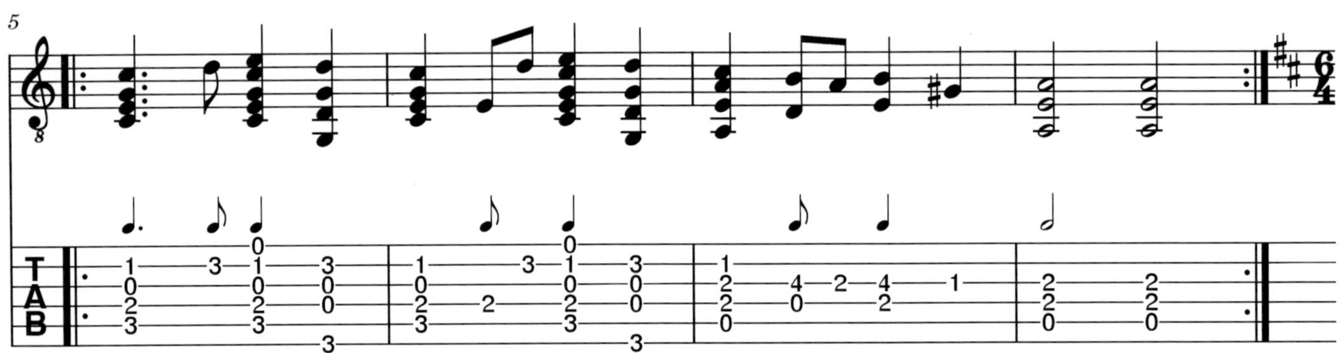

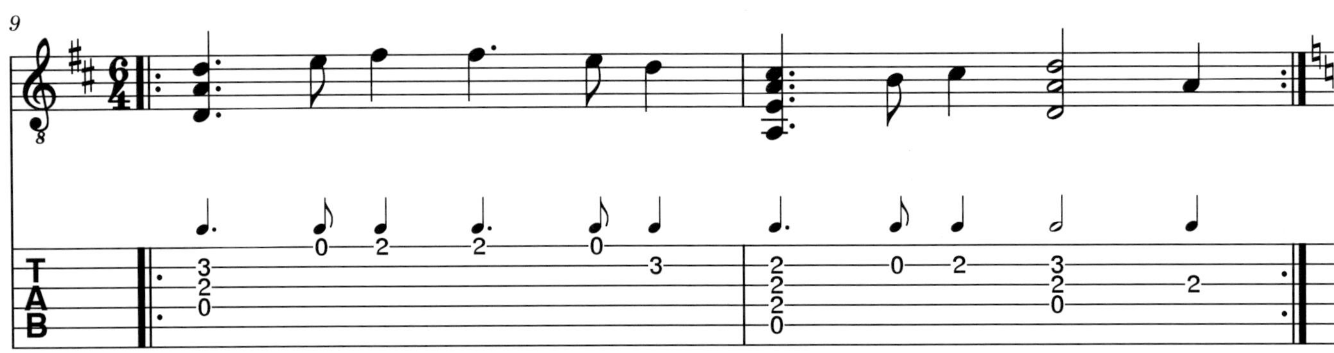

What if a Day

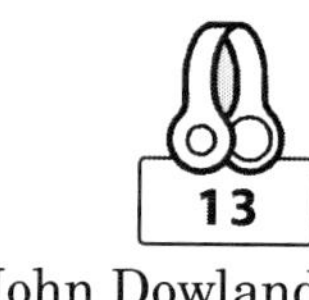

Arranged by
Rob MacKillop

John Dowland

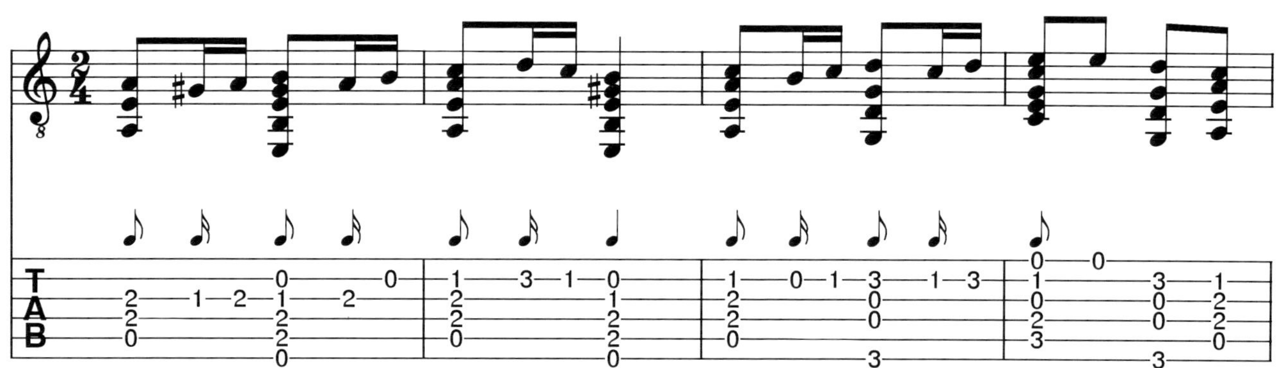

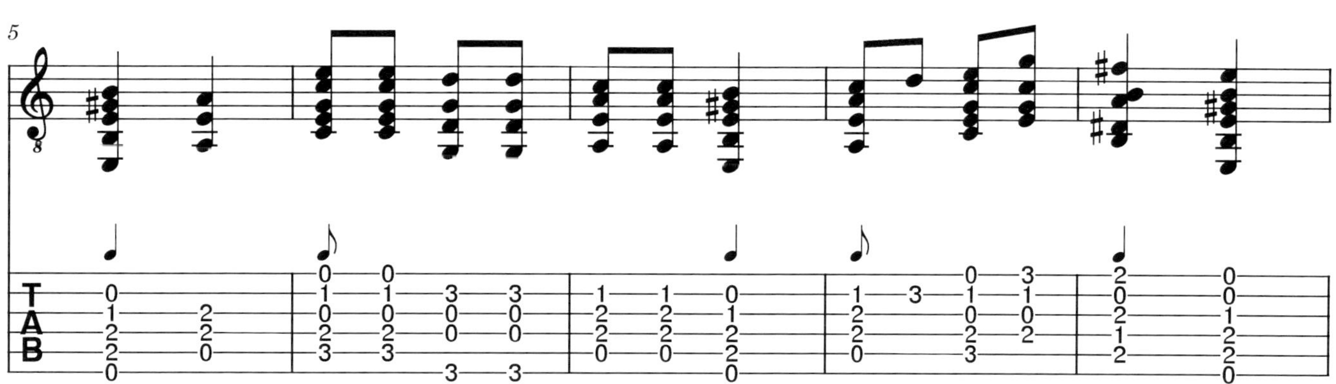

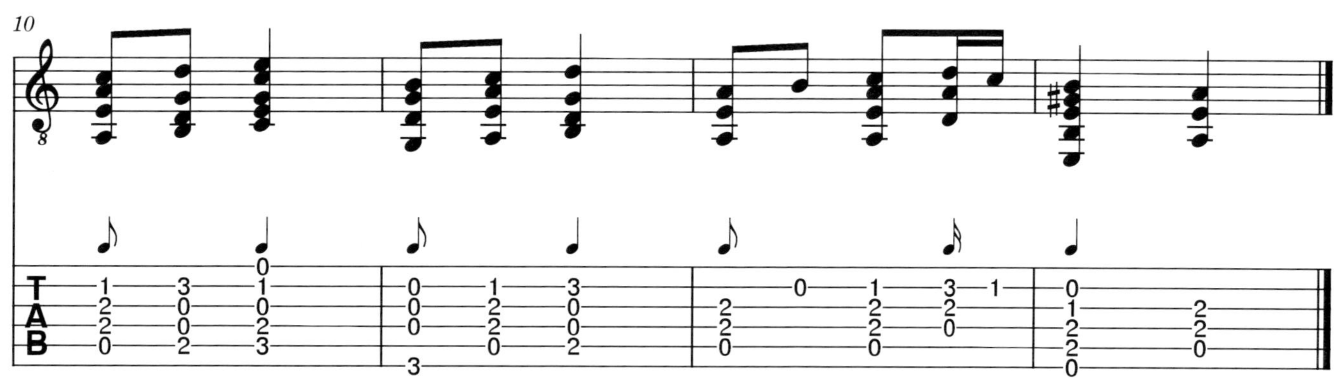

Fantasia 2

14

Arranged by
Rob MacKillop

Benedict de Drusina

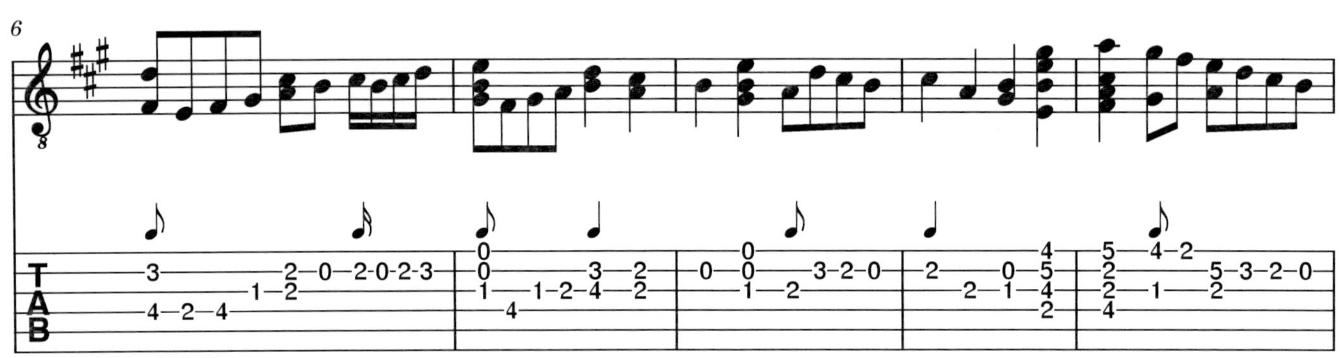

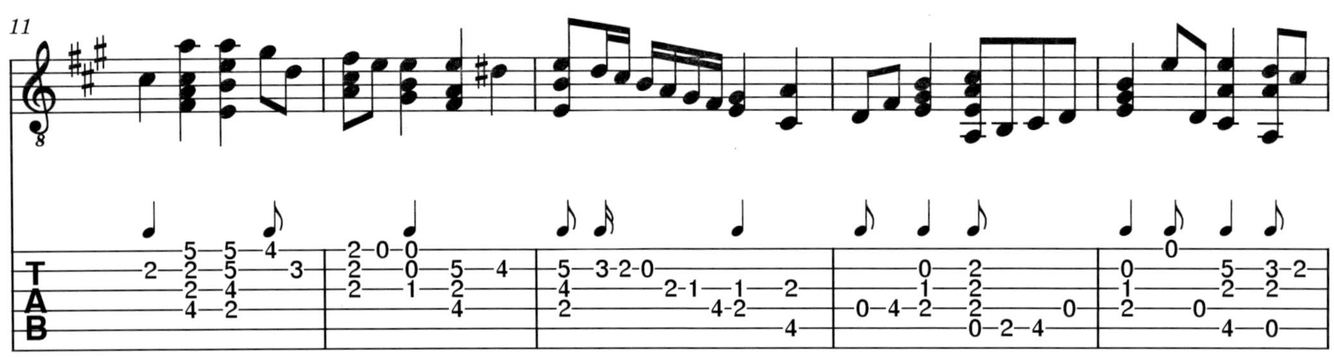

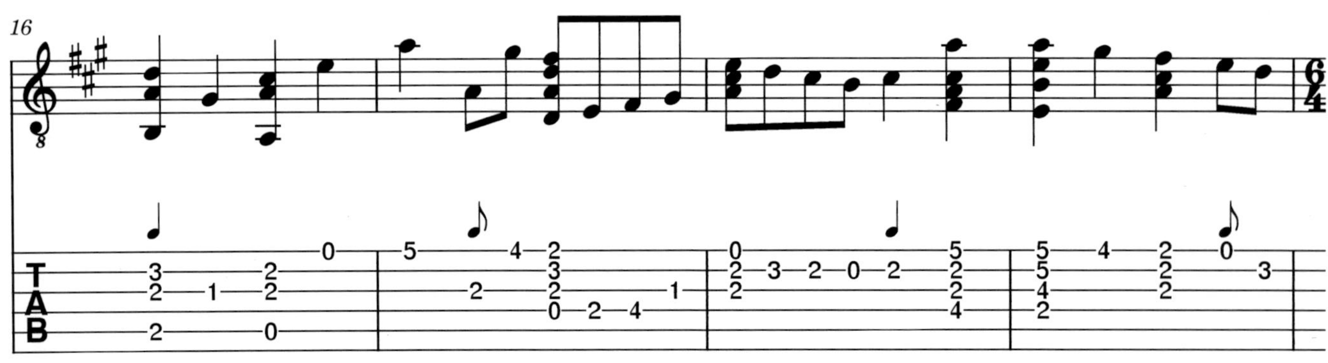

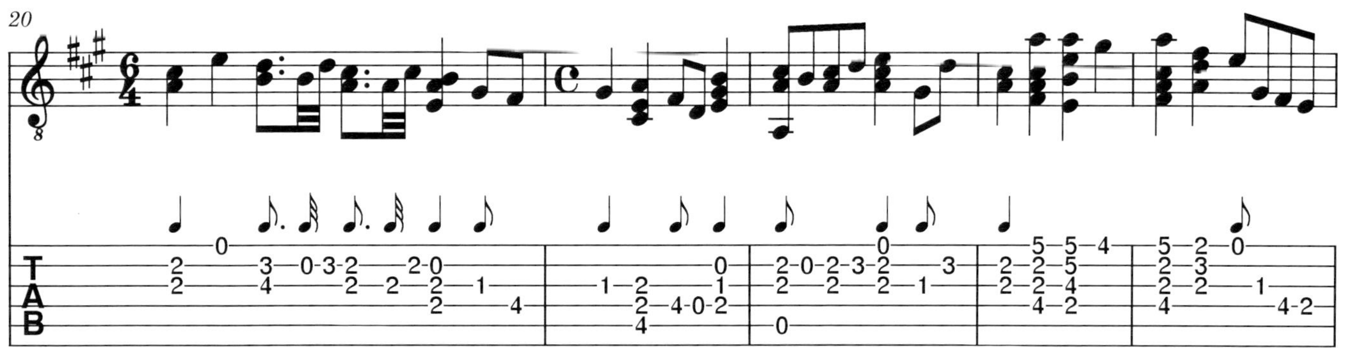

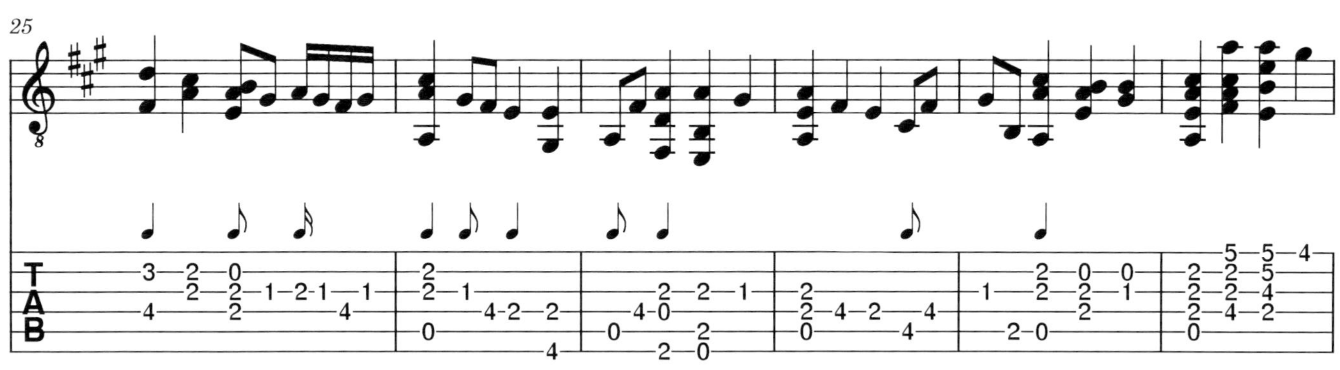

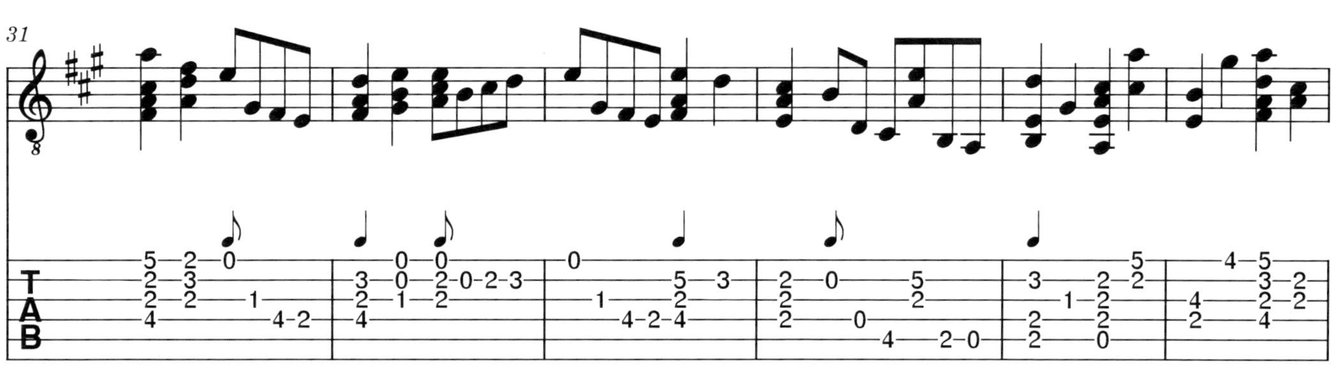

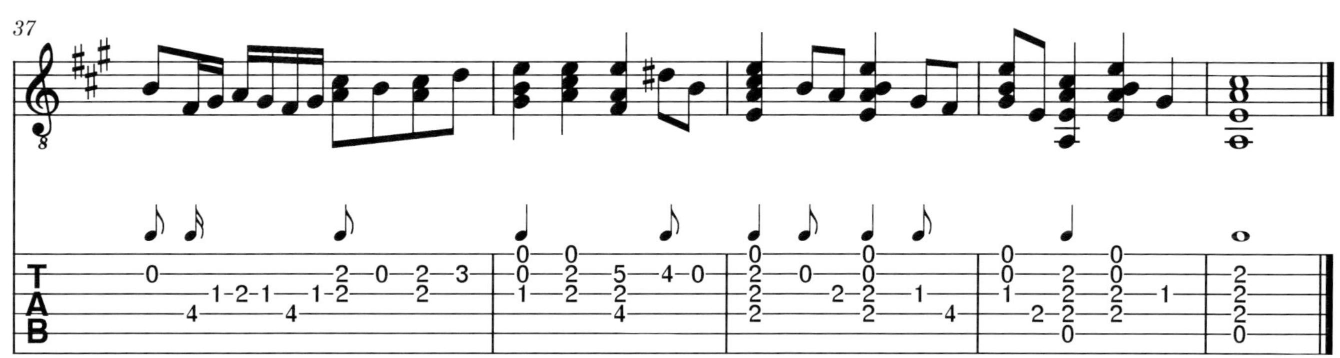

Alman

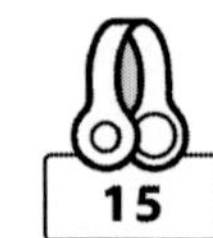

Arranged by
Rob MacKillop

Robert Johnson

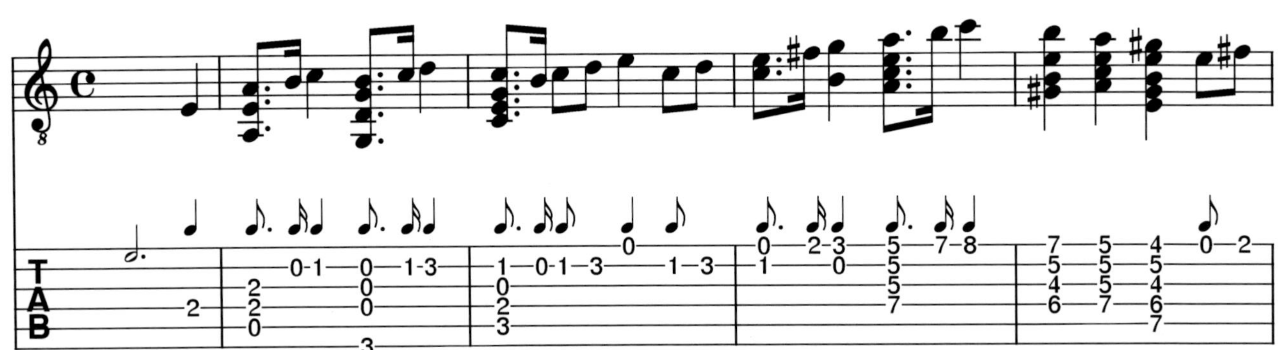

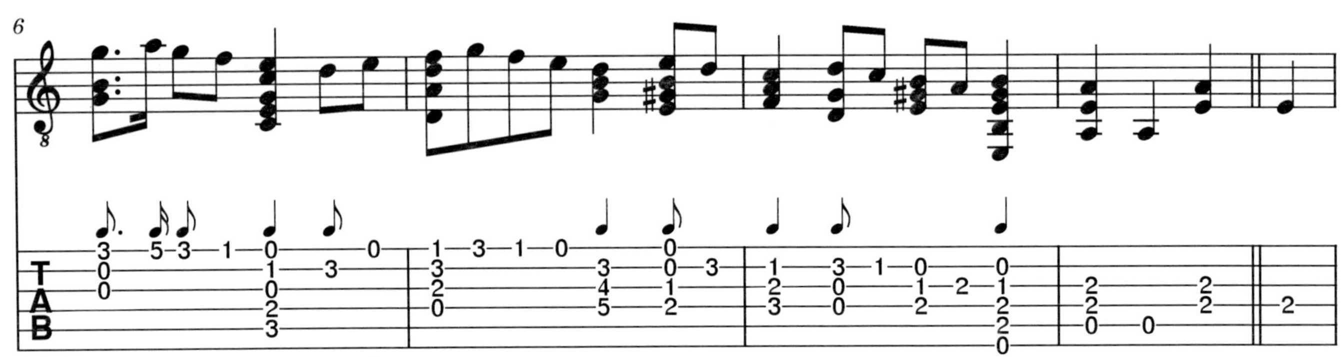

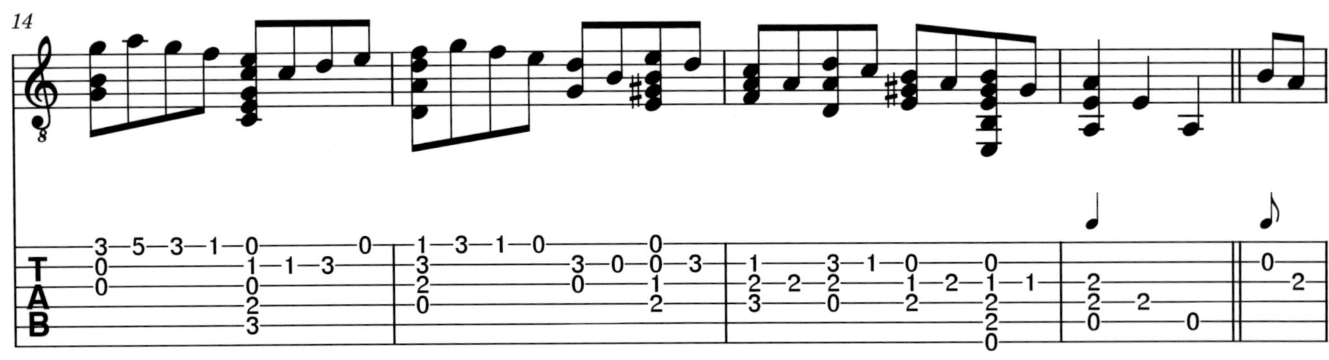

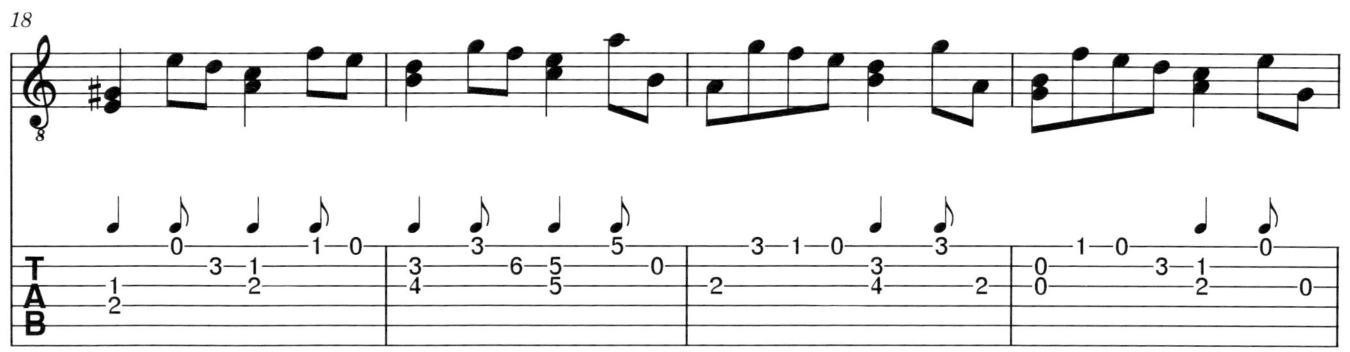
18
TAB

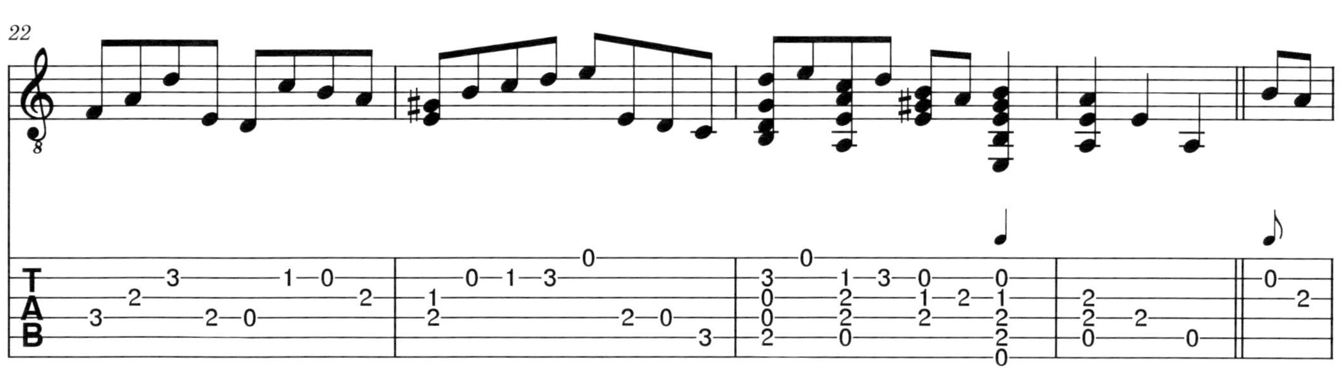
22
TAB

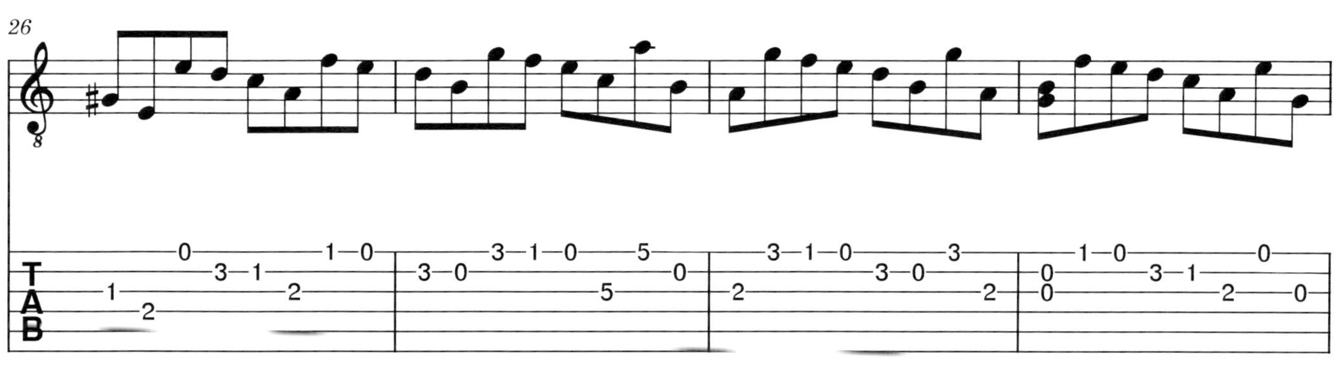
26
TAB

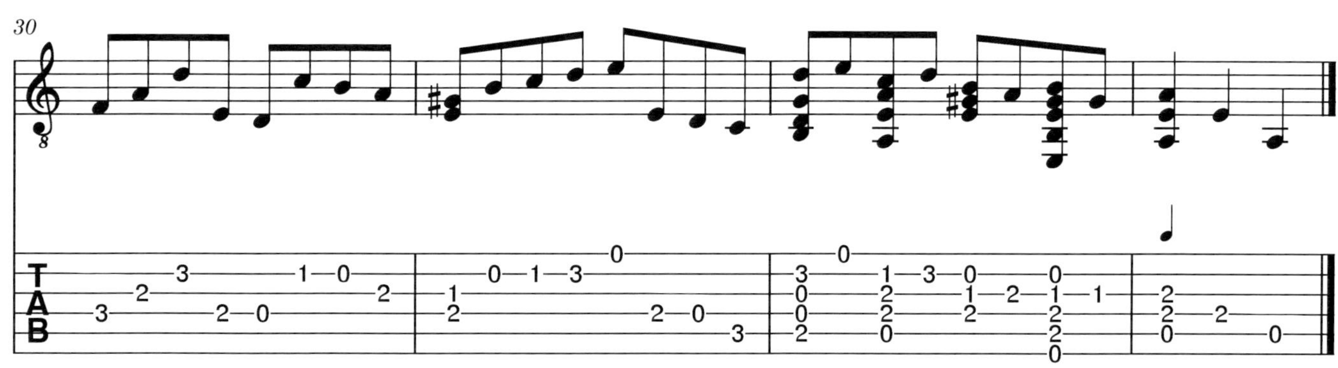
30
TAB

Ricercare 1

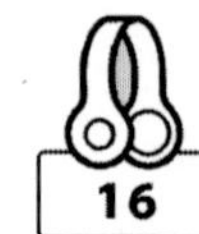

Arranged by
Rob MacKillop

Francesco Spinacino

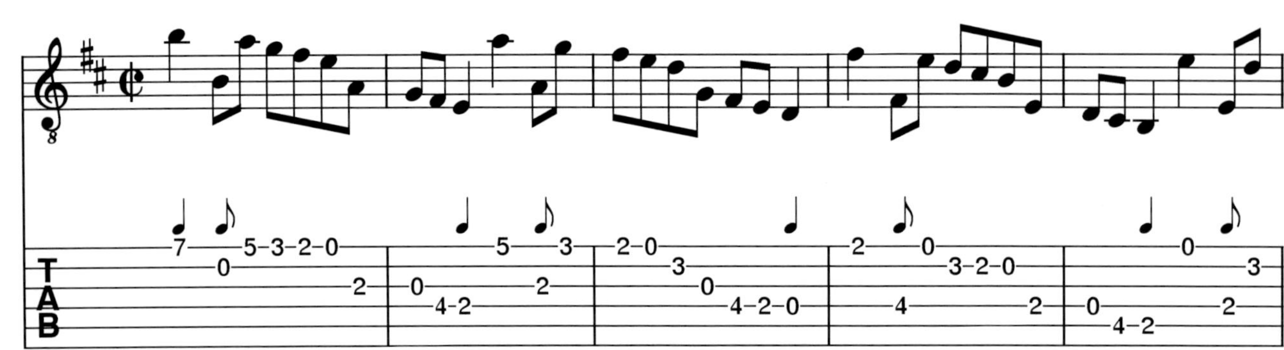

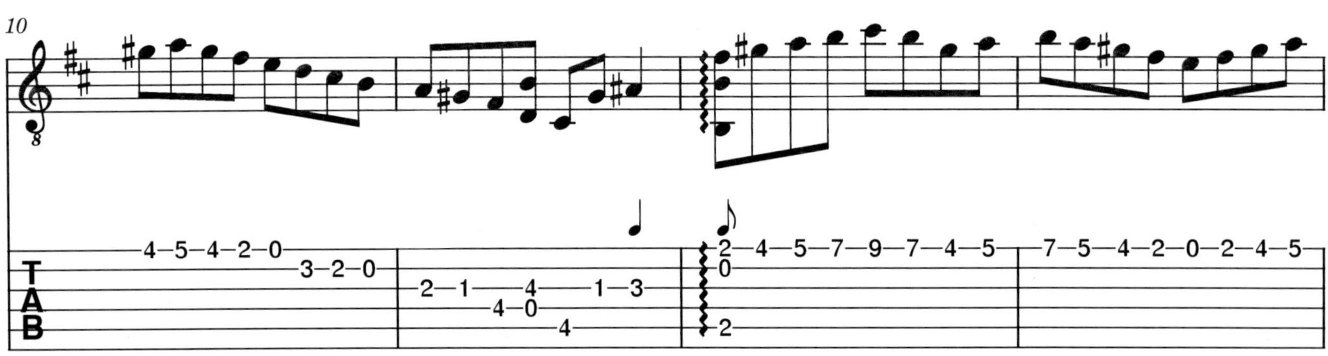

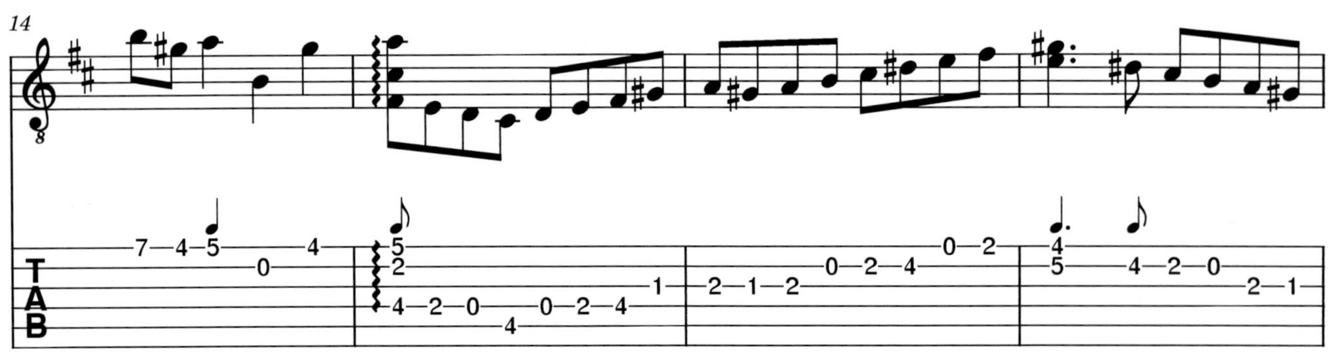

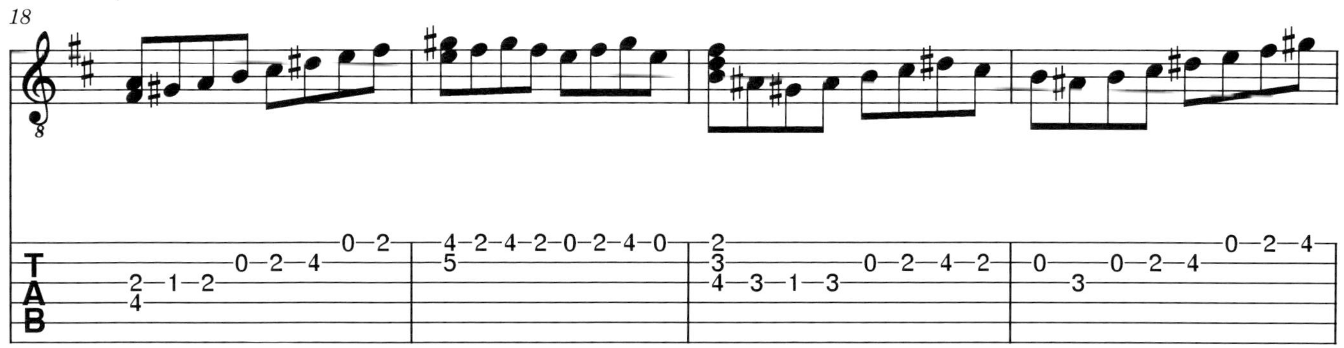
18
T
A
B

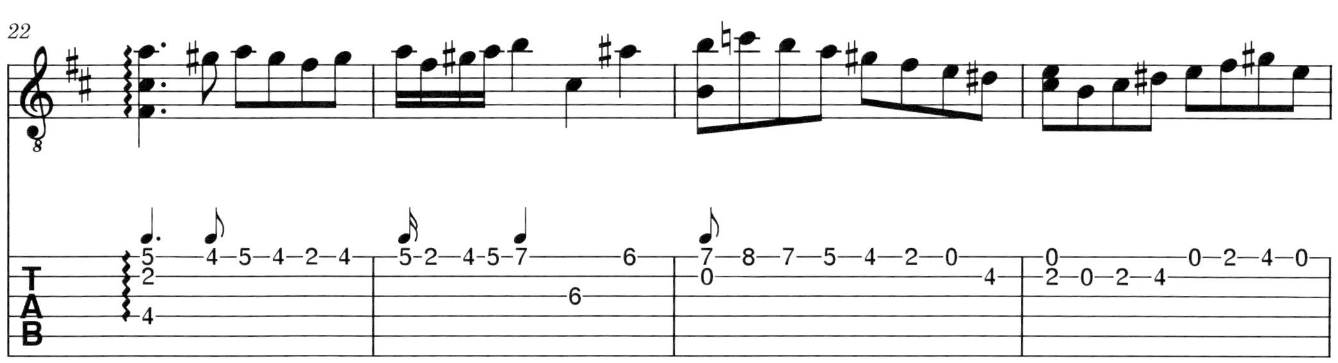
22
T
A
B

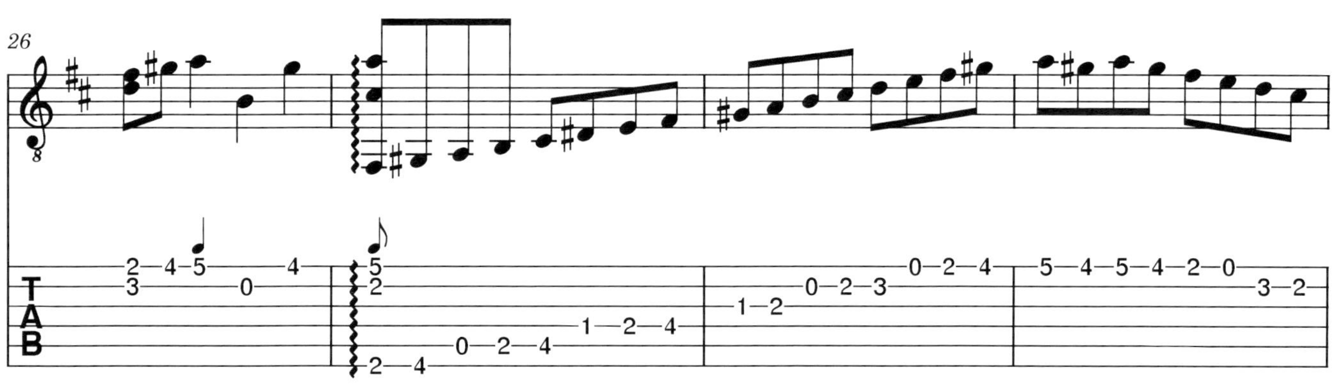
26
T
A
B

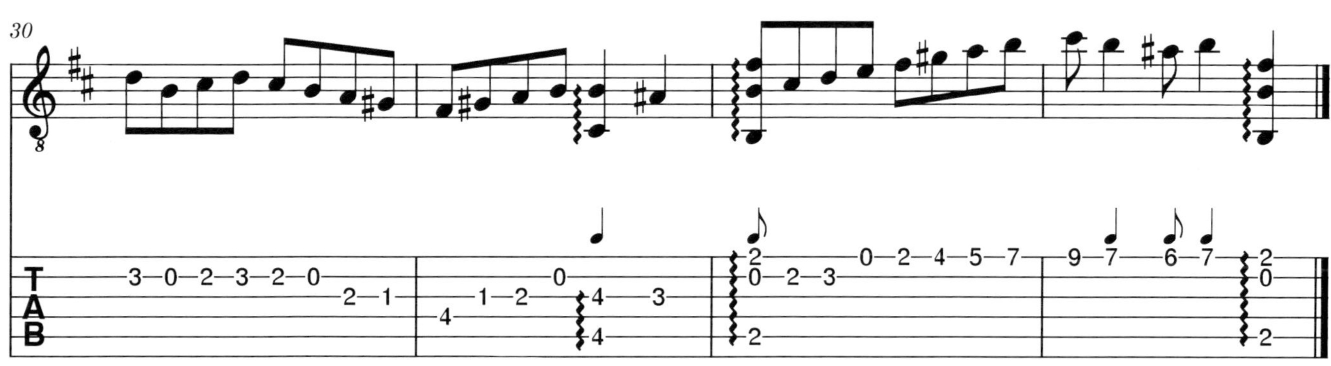
30
T
A
B

Ricercare 2

1507

Arranged by
Rob MacKillop

Francesco Spinacino

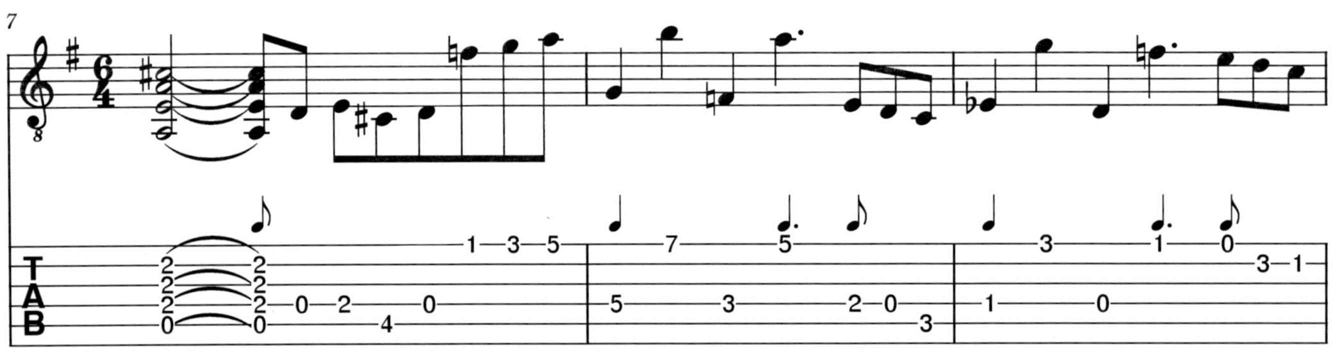

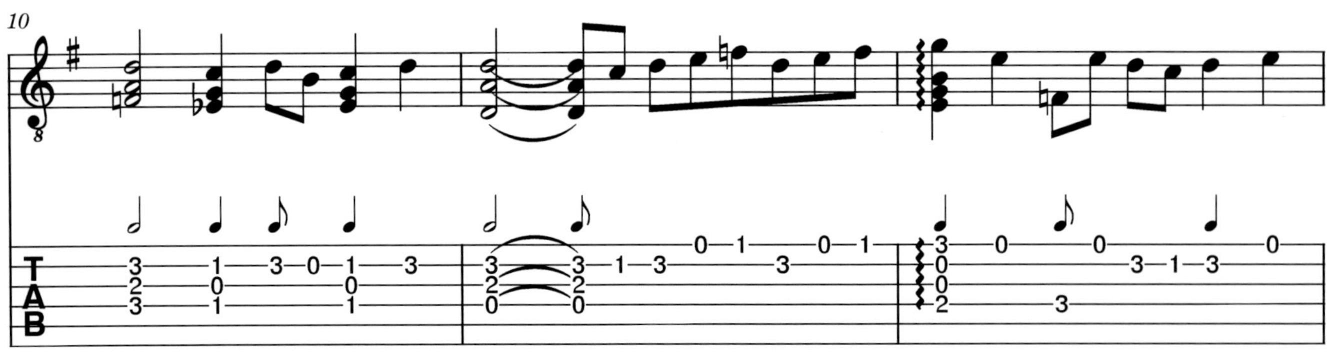

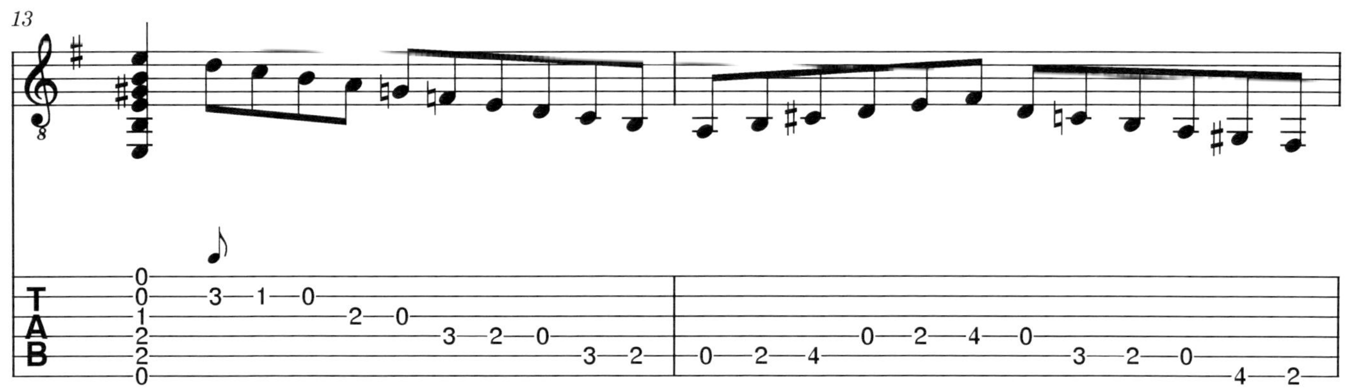

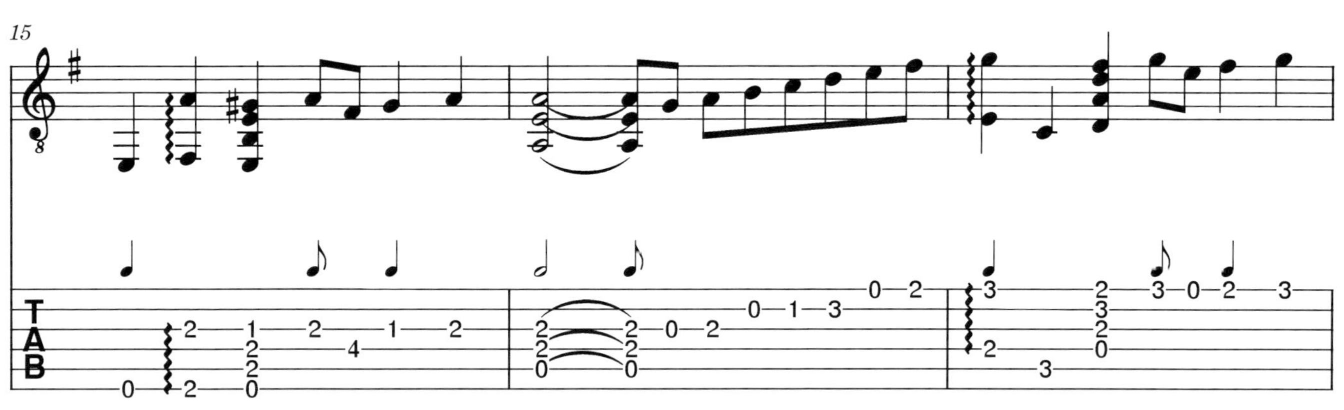

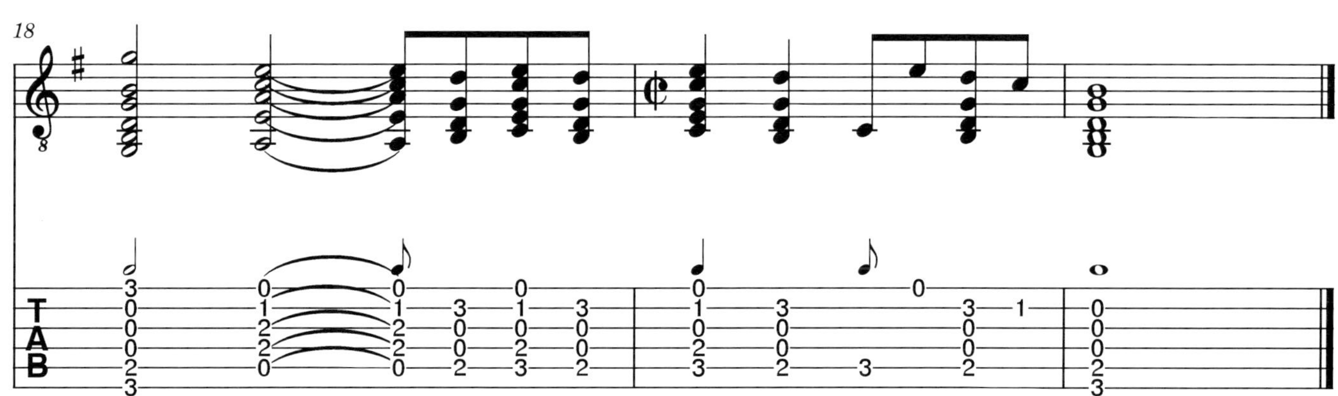

Fantasia in Em

Arranged by
Rob MacKillop

S. L. Weiss

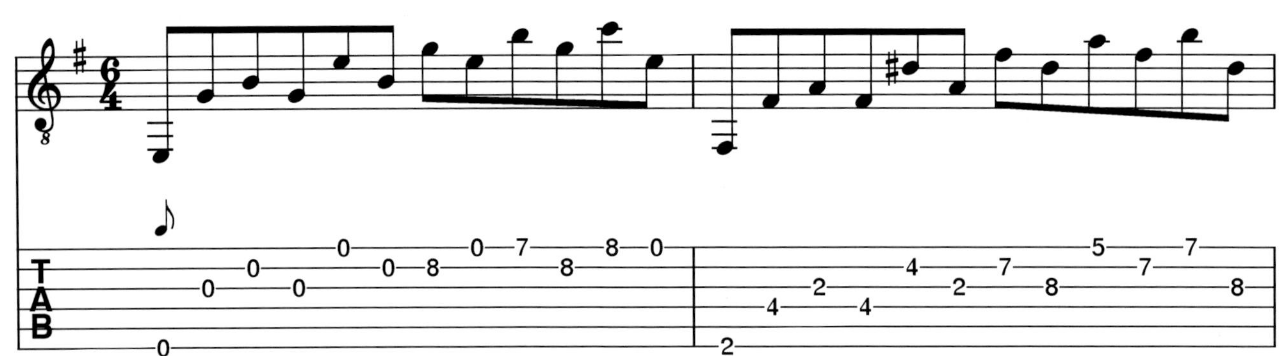

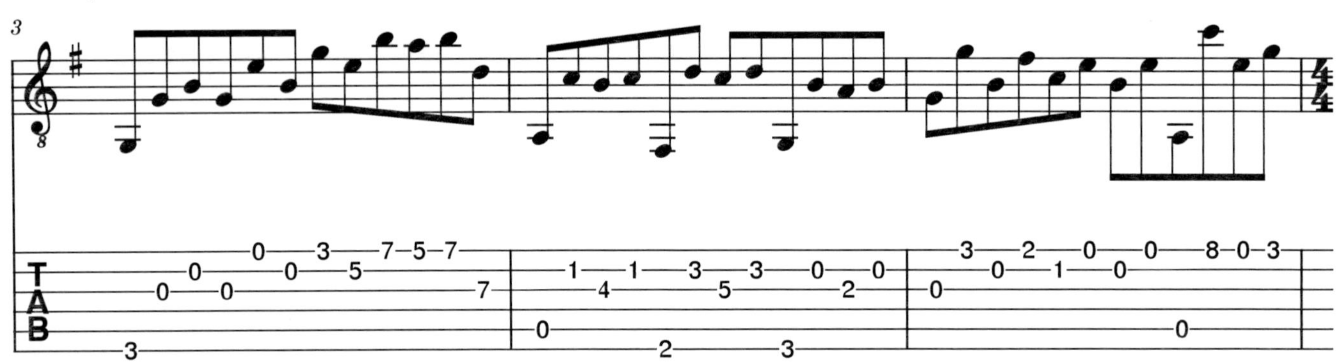

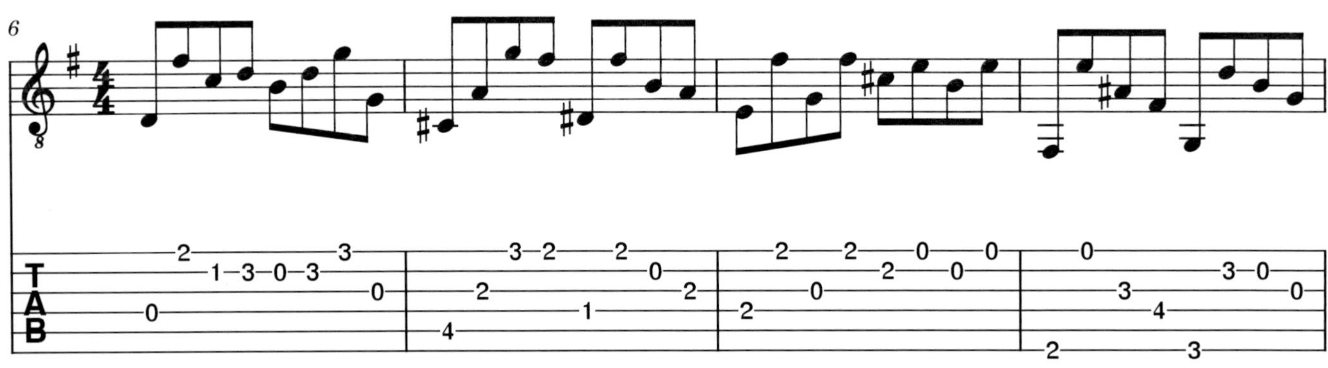

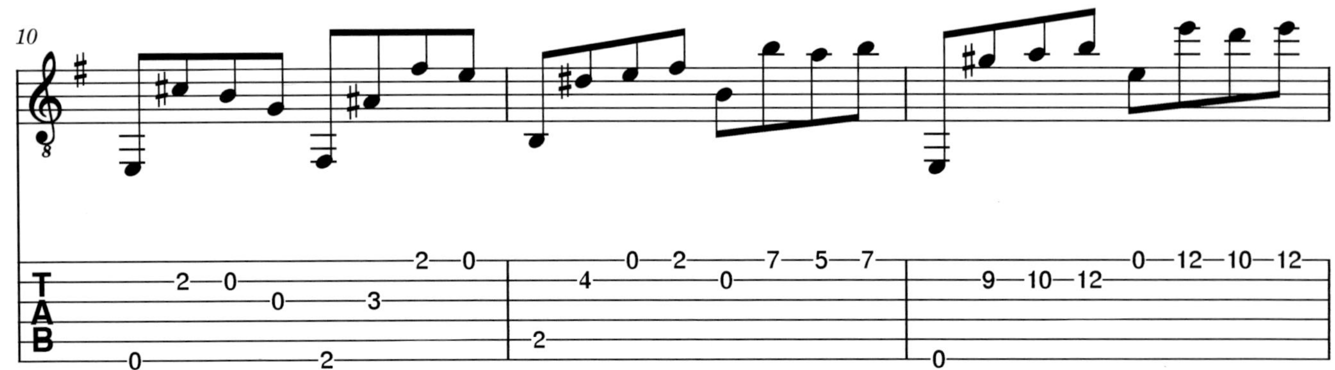

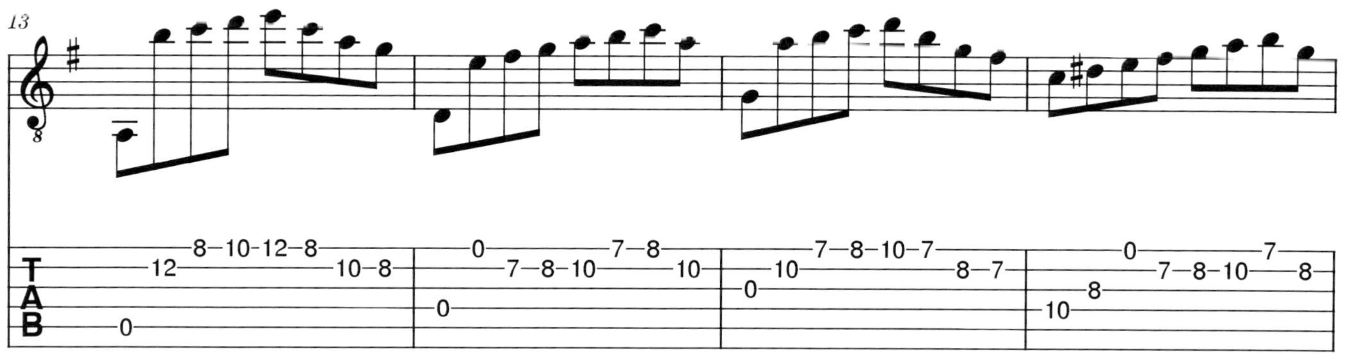
13
TAB

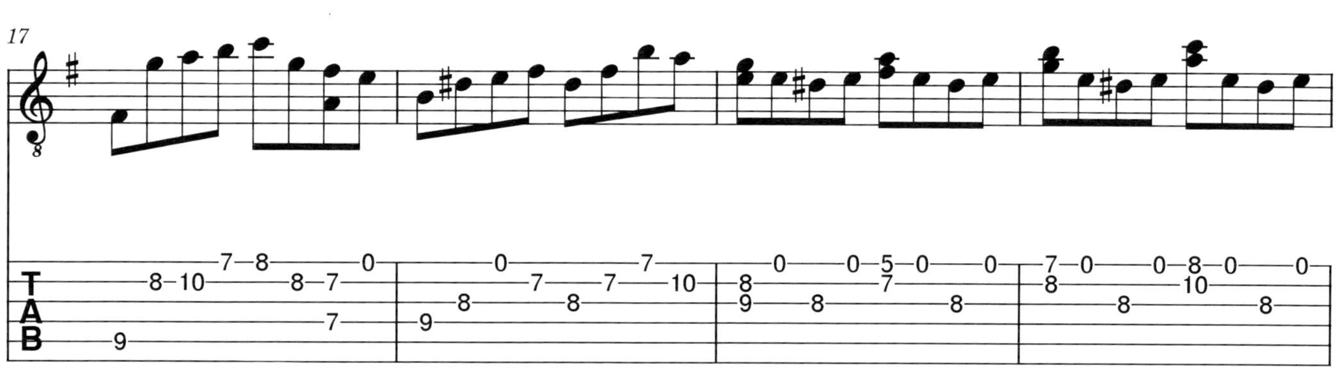
17
TAB

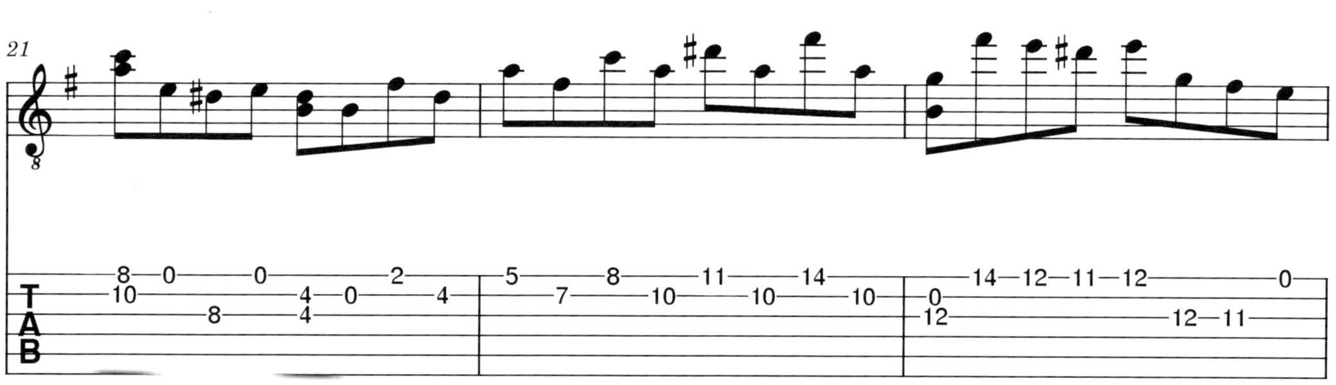
21
TAB

24
TAB

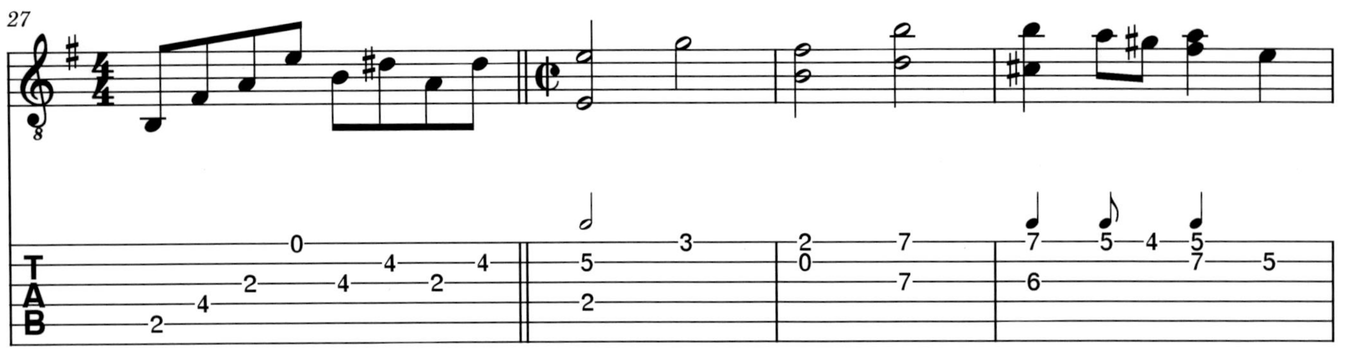
27
T
A
B
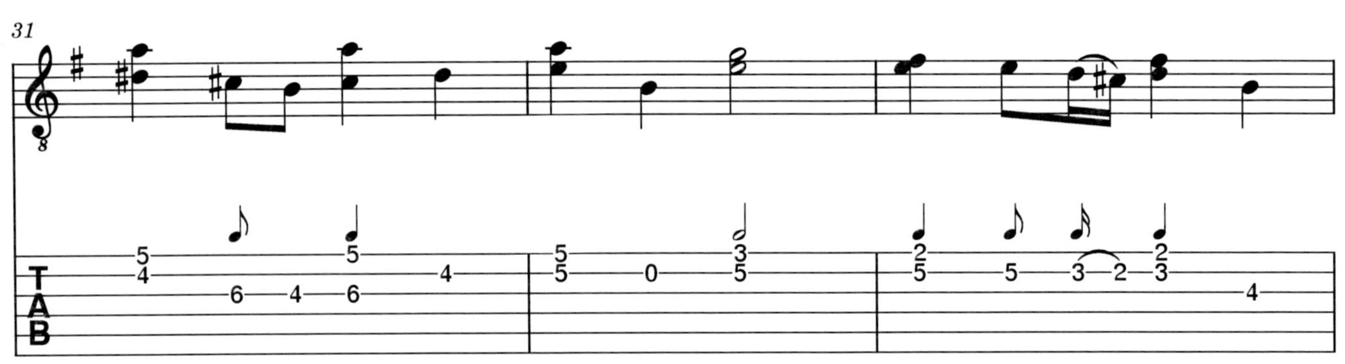
31
T
A
B
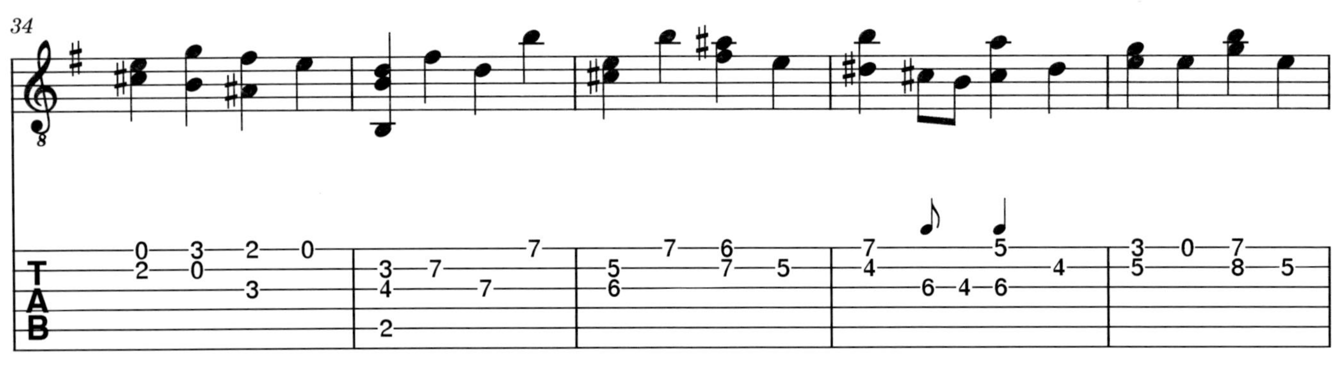
34
T
A
B

39
T
A
B

43
TAB
3 5 7 3
0
0
5 10
7 7
7
0 5 7 5
8 5 8
6
3
7 0 0
7 7
0
1
2 7 5
4

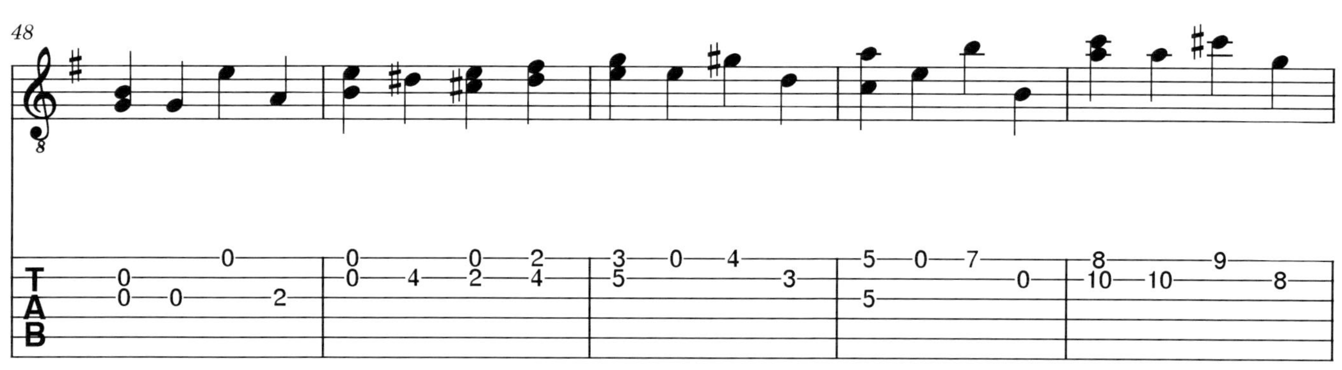
48
TAB
0
0
0 0 2
0 0 2
0 4 2 4
3 0 4
5 3
5 0 7
0
5
8 9
10 10 8

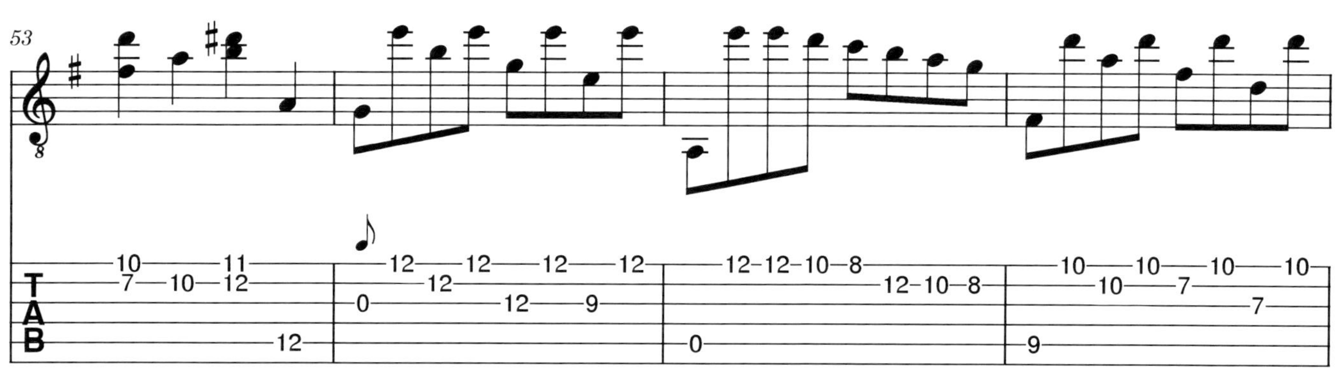
53
TAB
10 11
7 10 12
12
12 12 12 12
12
0 12 9
12 12 10 8
12 10 8
0
10 10 10 10
10 7
7
9

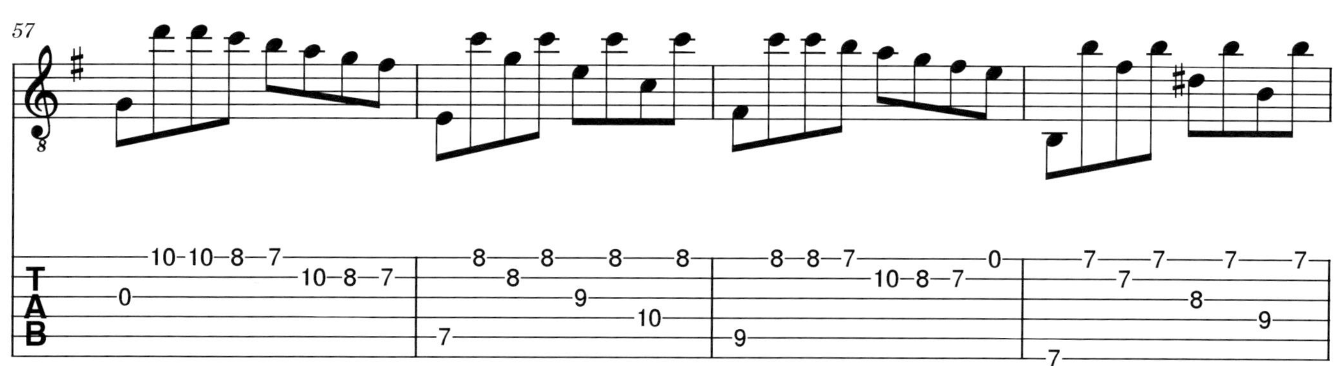
57
TAB
10 10 8 7
10 8 7
0
8 8 8 8
8
9
10
7
8 8 7
10 8 7 0
9
7 7 7 7
7
8
9
7

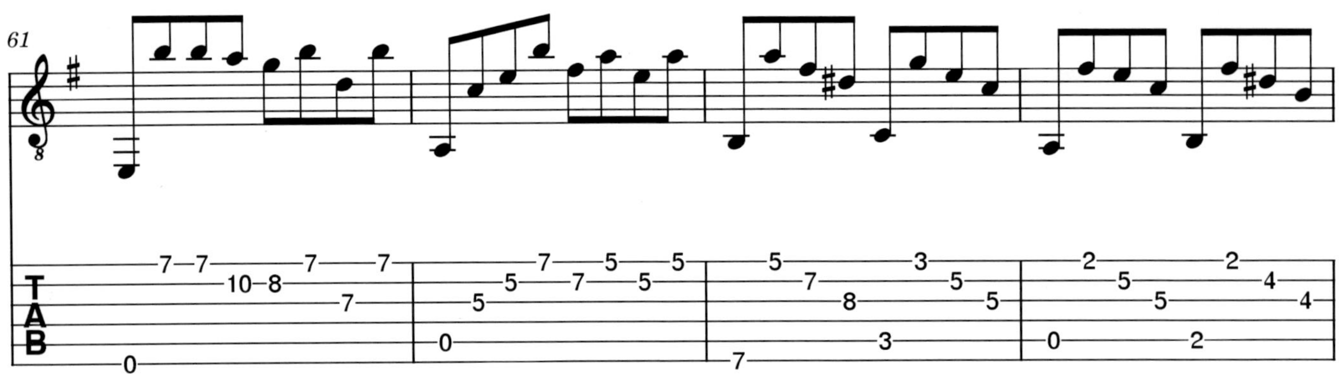
61

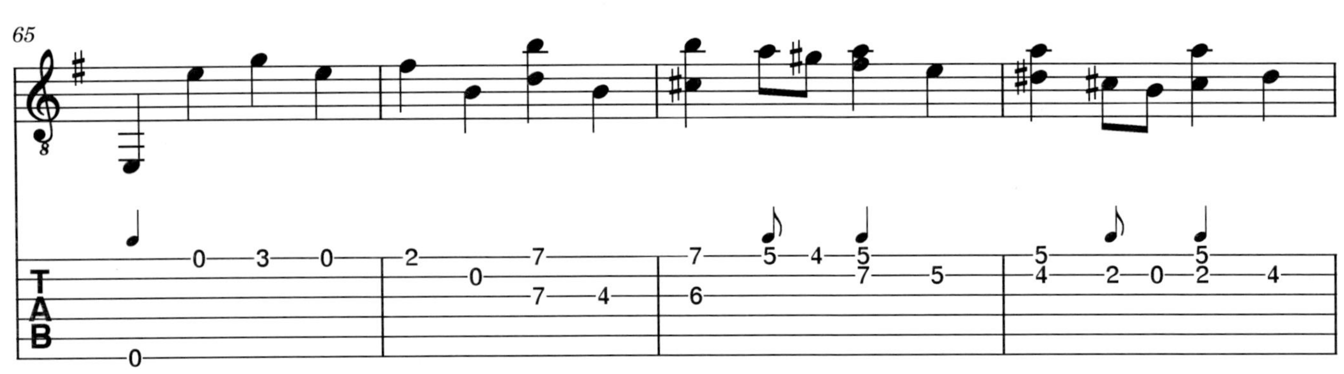
65

69

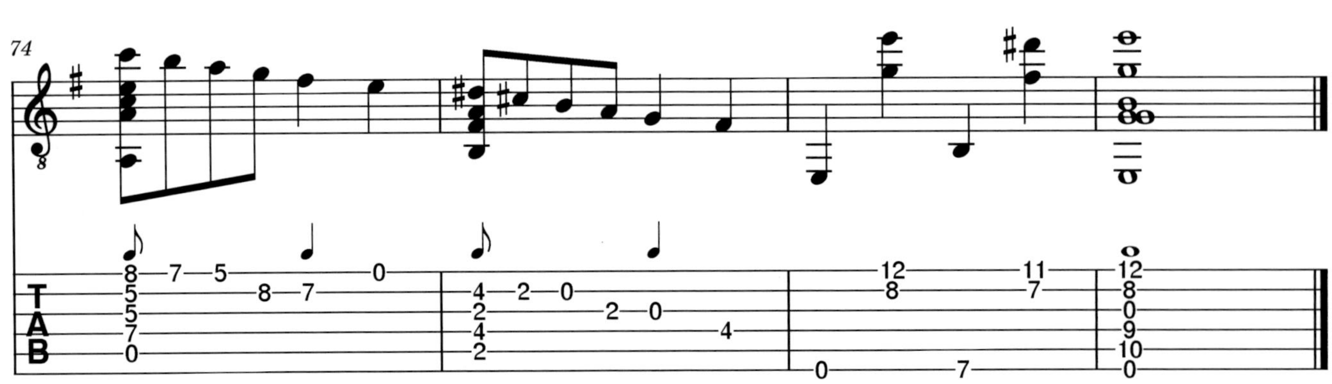
74

Prelude in Em

[Originally Dm]

Arranged by
Rob MacKillop

S. L. Weiss

19

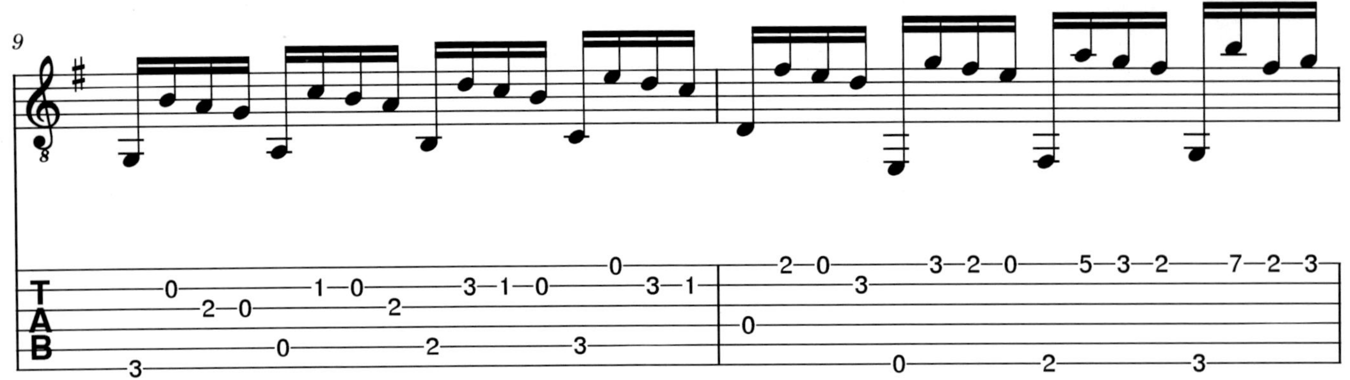
9

11

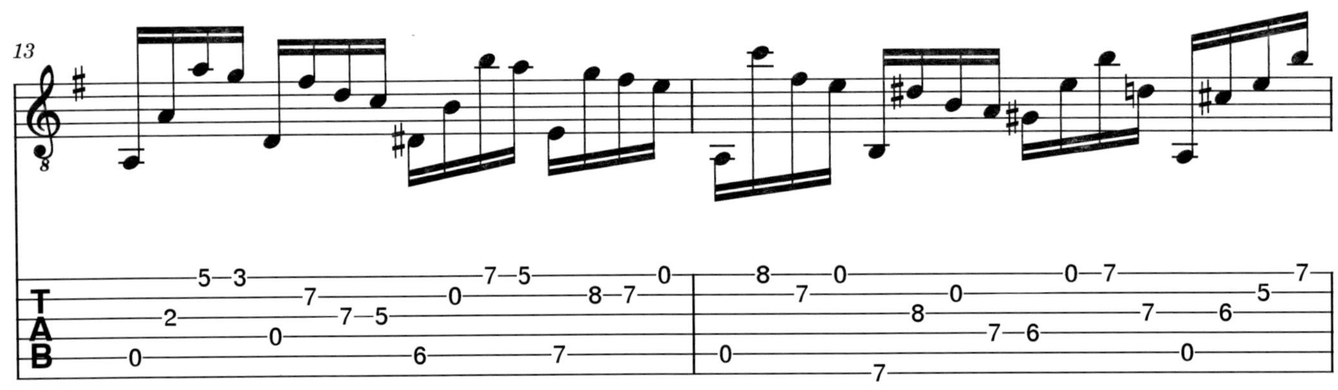
13

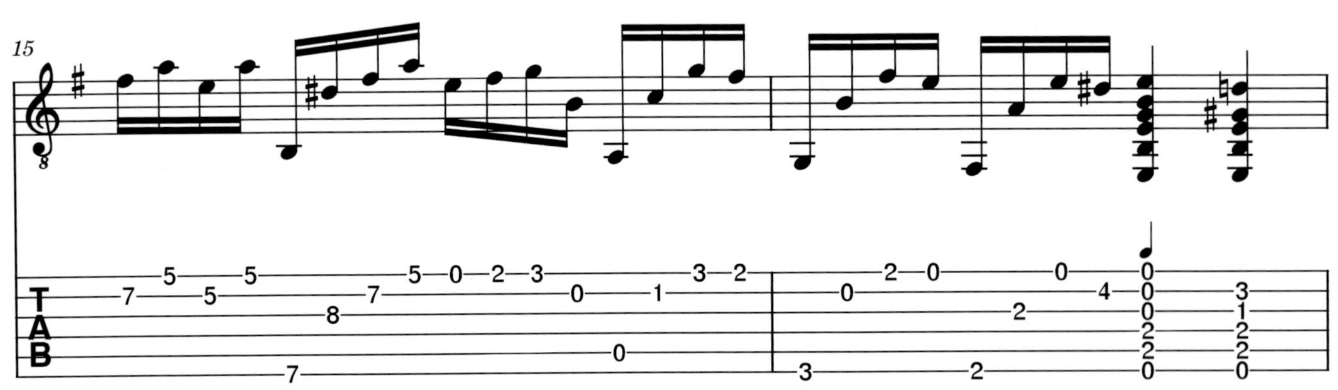
15

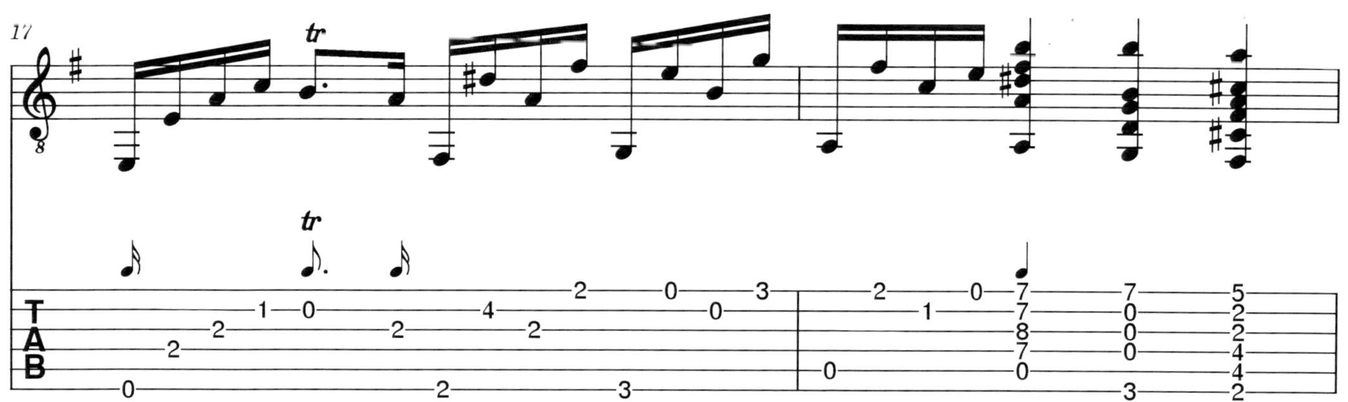
17
tr
tr

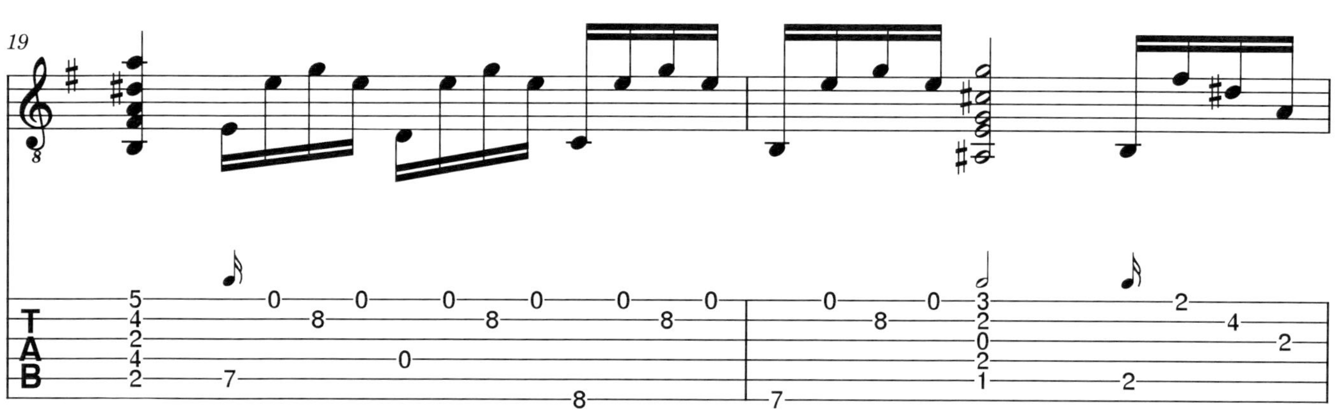
19

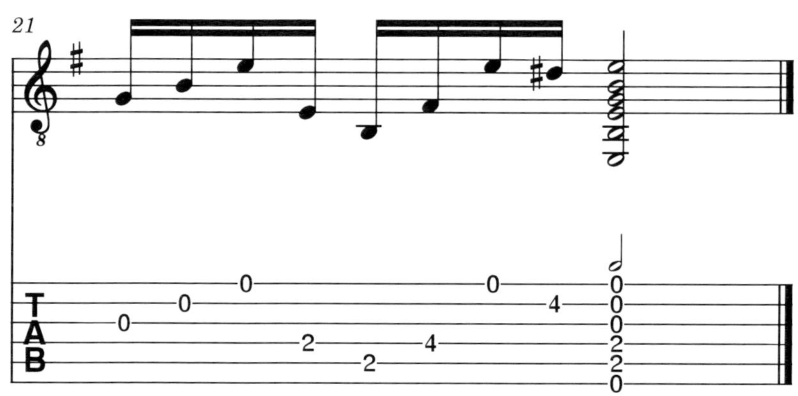
21

Tombeau sur la Mort de M. Comte de Logy

Arranged by Rob MacKillop

20

S. L. Weiss

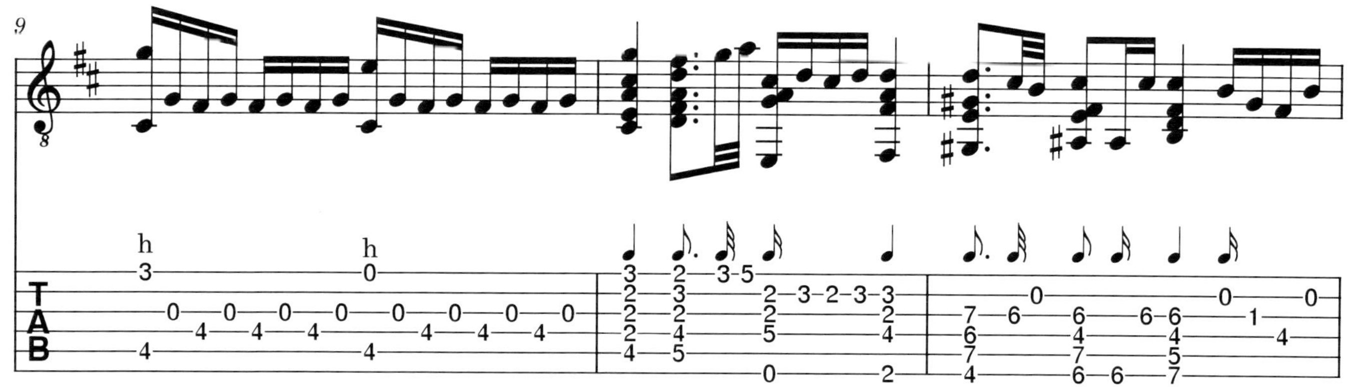
9
h
h
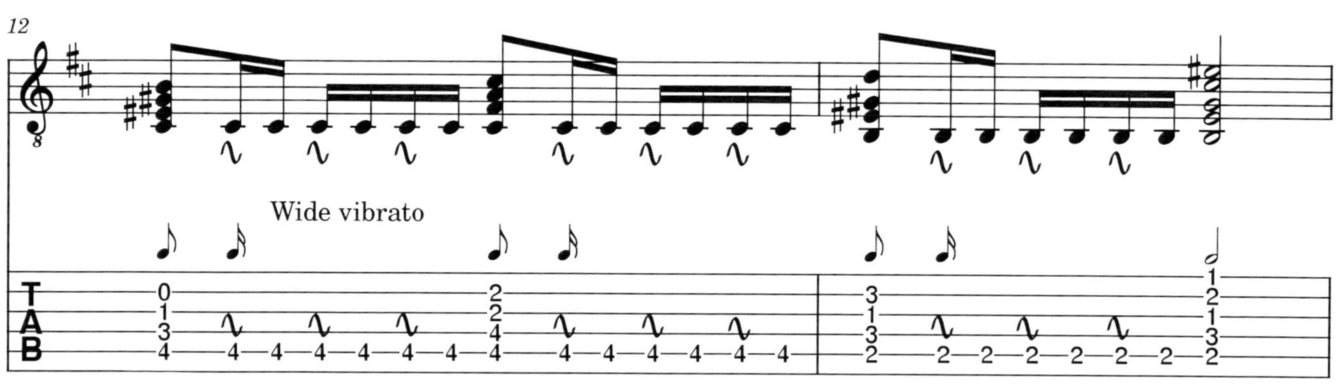
12
Wide vibrato

14
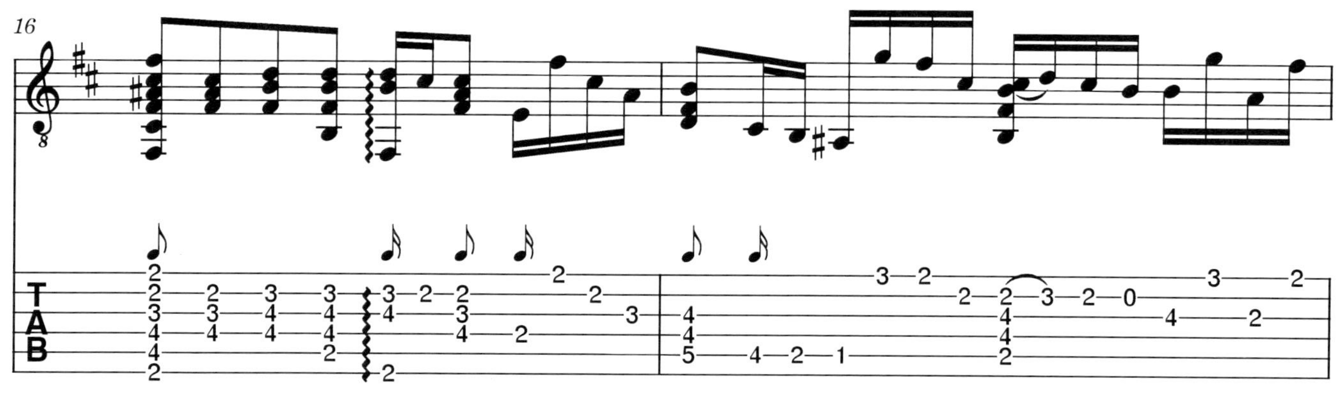
16

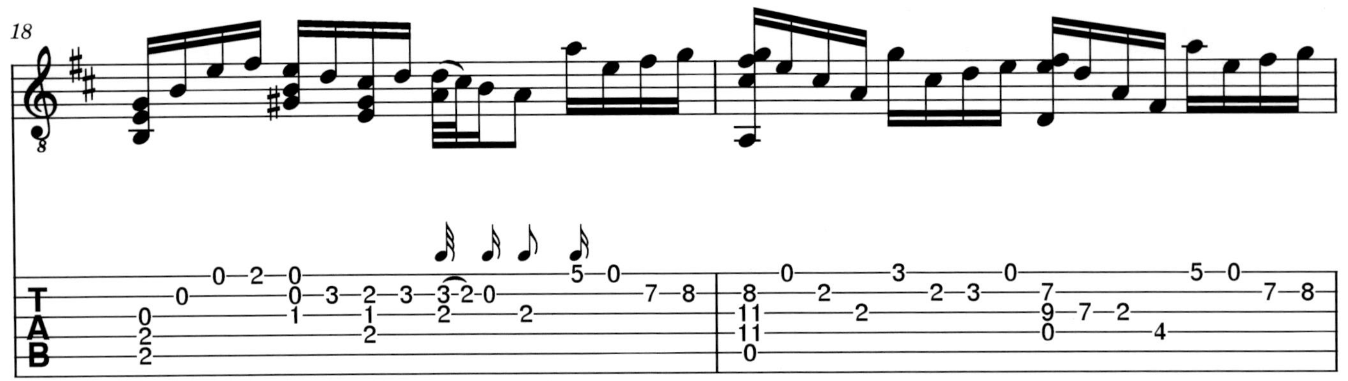

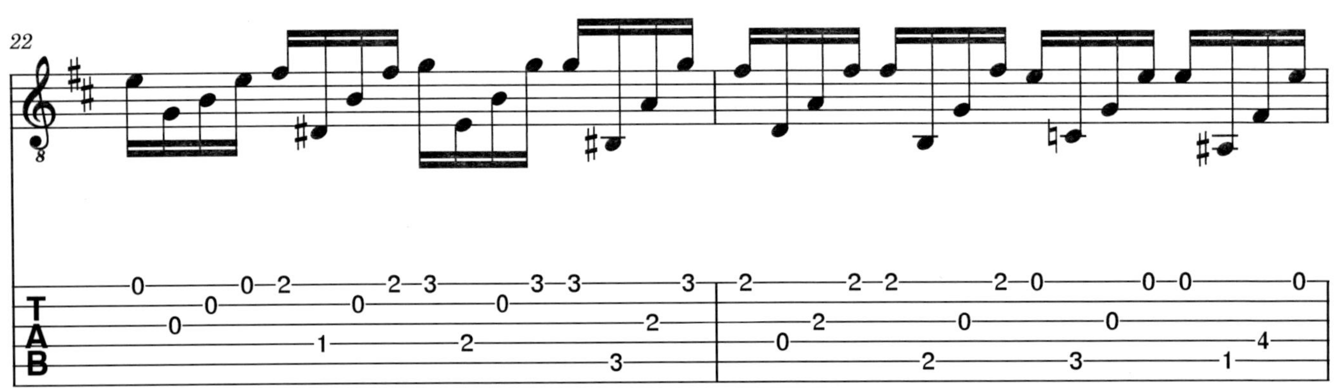

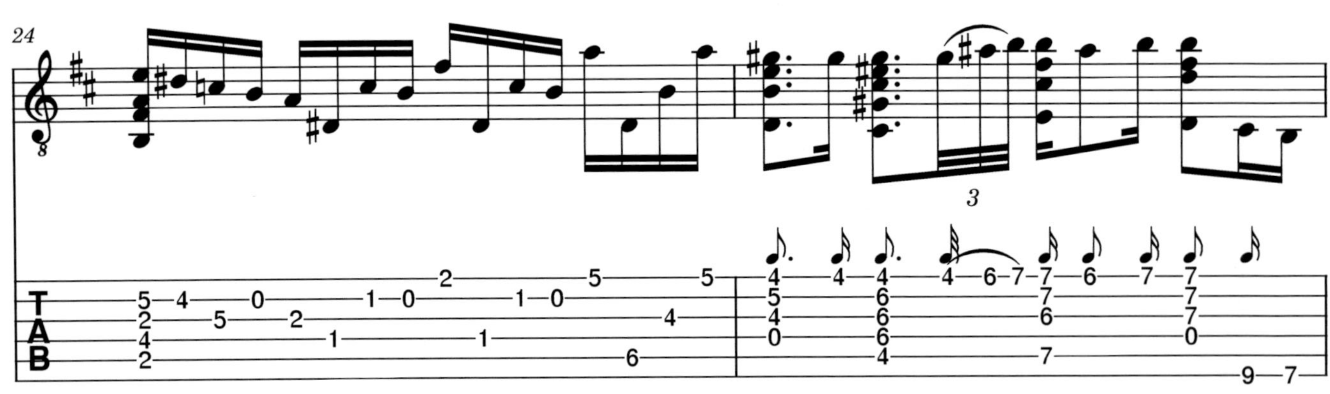

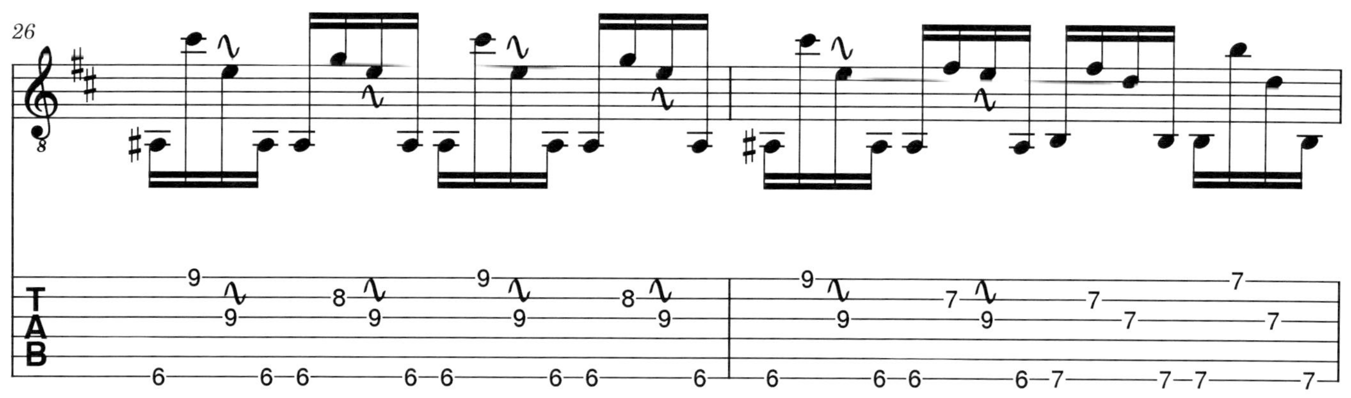
26
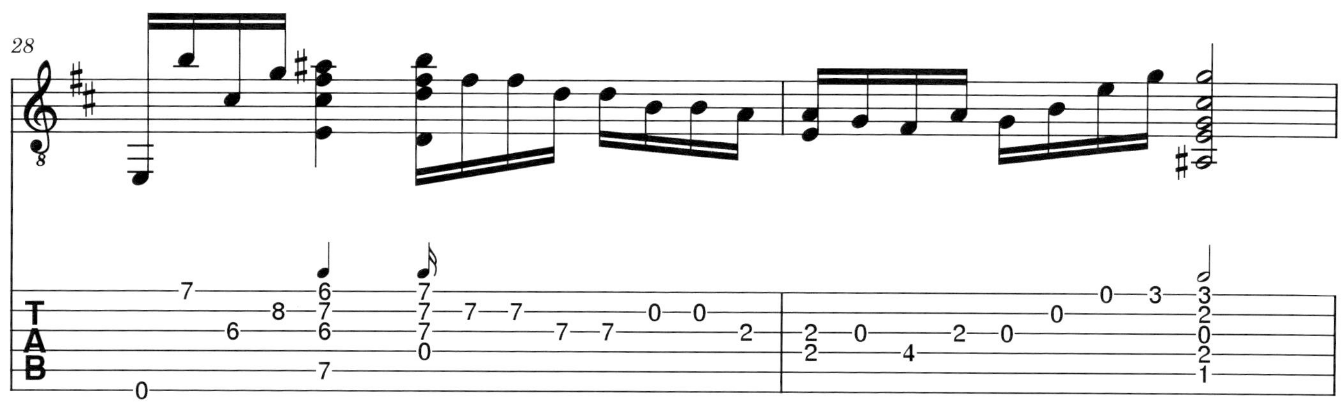
28
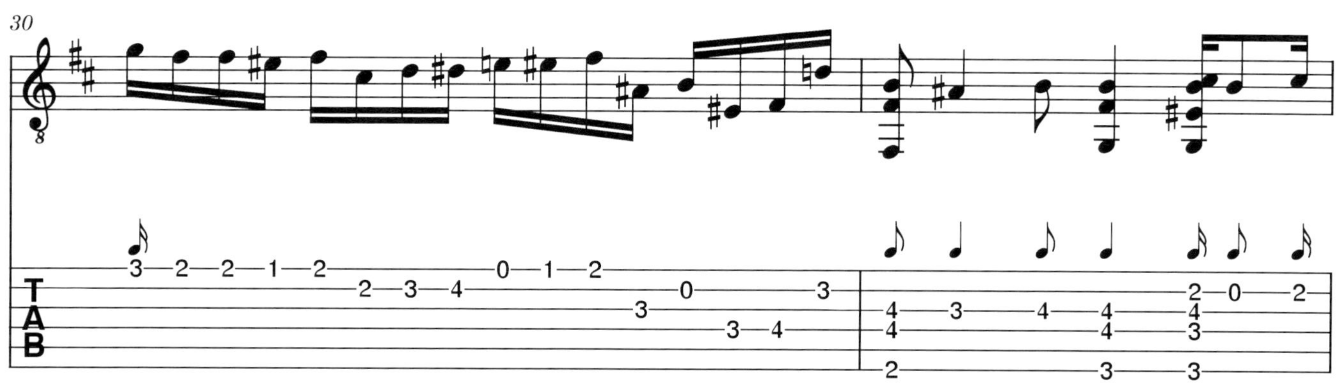
30
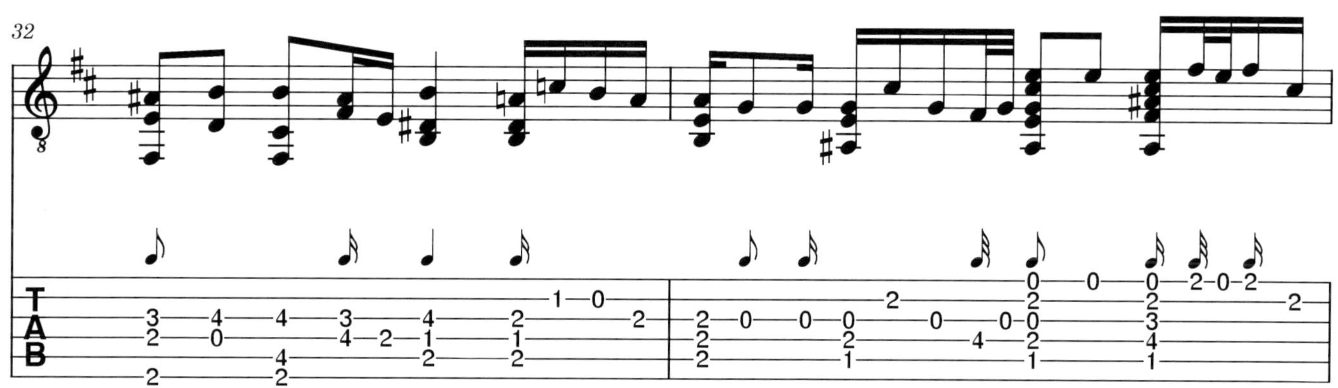
32

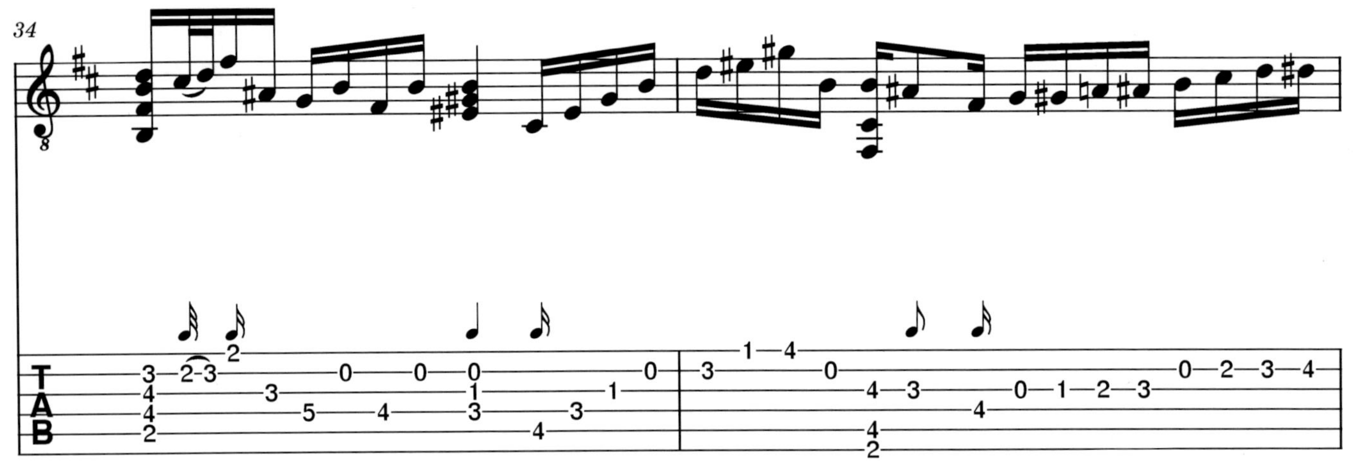
34
T
A
B

36
T
A
B

Rob MacKillop

"One of Scotland's finest musicians" ***Celtic World***

"A top-drawer player" ***Early Music Today***

"MacKillop displays dazzling virtuosity...the playing is exceptionally musical." ***Sounding Strings***

Rob MacKillop has recorded eight CDs of historical music, three of which reached the Number One position in the Scottish Classical Music Chart. In 2001 he was awarded a Churchill Fellowship for his research into medieval Scottish music, which led him to study with Sufi musicians in Istanbul and Morocco. He broadcast an entire solo concert on BBC Radio 3 from John Smith's Square, London. He has presented academic papers at conferences in Portugal and Germany, and has been published many times. Rob has been active in both historical and contemporary music.

An experienced teacher (Royal Scottish Academy of Music, Napier University Edinburgh, etc) Rob now teaches people from around the world via Zoom from his home studio in Edinburgh. Contact can be made via his website, http://RobMacKillop.net

Other Recommended Mel Bay Plectrum Guitar Books

6 Pieces for Guitar Solo (Pritchard)
24 Pieces for Guitar by Gilbert Isbin
25 Solos from the Unaccompanied Partitas of J. S. Bach (W. Bay/Leonard)
Achieving Guitar Artistry: Concert Solos (W. Bay)
Achieving Guitar Artistry: Contemporary Baroque (W. Bay)
Achieving Guitar Artistry: Linear Guitar Etudes (W. Bay)
Achieving Guitar Artistry: Lyrical Etudes (Pennanen)
Achieving Guitar Artistry: Preludes, Sonatas & Nocturnes (W. Bay)
Acoustic Guitar Portraits: Duets (W. Bay)
Christmas Guitar Portraits (Duets) (W. Bay)
Classics for Electric Guitar (Kiefer)
Devotion: Sacred Solos for Guitar (W. Bay)
Electric Baroque Guitar (Kiefer)
Folio of Graded Guitar Solos (M. Bay)
Graded Guitar Duets (M. Bay)
Guitar Duets on Great Classic Themes (Hendrickson/Orzeck)
Guitar Images (W. Bay)
Guitar Picking Tunes - An Early American Christmas (W. Bay)
Guitar Picking Tunes - Beautiful Airs and Ballads of the British Isles (W. Bay)
Guitar Picking Tunes - Beautiful American Airs and Ballads (W. Bay)
Guitar Picking Tunes - Blues & Jazz Jam Tunes (W. Bay)
Guitar Picking Tunes - Christmas in the British Isles (W. Bay)
Guitar Picking Tunes - Classical Gems (W. Bay)
Guitar Picking Tunes - Early Music Gems (W. Bay)
Guitar Picking Tunes - Fun Solos to Play (W. Bay)
Guitar Picking Tunes - Celtic Gems (W. Bay)
Guitar Picking Tunes - Celtic Hymns and Sacred Songs (W. Bay)
Guitar Picking Tunes - Jumpin' Guitar Jam Tunes (W. Bay)
Guitar Picking Tunes - Lyrical Gospel Solos (W. Bay)
Guitar Picking Tunes - Melodious Etudes (W. Bay)
Guitar Picking Tunes - Old-Time Music Gems (W. Bay)
Guitar Picking Tunes - Sacred Songs of Early America (W. Bay)
Guitar Picking Tunes - Songs of Faith (W. Bay)
Guitar Tangos (W. Bay)
Lively Guitar Tunes (W. Bay)
Mastering the Guitar Duets (W. Bay/M. Christiansen)
Masters of the Plectrum Guitar (Multiple Authors)
Mozart for Electric Guitar (Kiefer)
One Guitar, Many Styles (Finn)
Sal Salvadore Collection of Classic Solos for Pick-Style Guitar
The Christmas Gig Book for Pick-Style Guitar (Coppola)
Traditional Music of the British Isles for Electric Guitar (Berthoud)
Wedding Music for Pick-Style Guitar (Coppola)
The William Bay Collection - Plectrum Guitar Solo Anthology
The William Bay Collection - Sacred Guitar Solo Anthology

WWW.MELBAY.COM